By Way Of Introduction

We suggest that readers familiar with Sidney J. Parnes' work read the following in order: **Foreword** (p. xi), **Prologue** (p. xiii), **Reflections** (p. xvi).

If you are not familiar with the author's work, we suggest that you commence with **Chapter One,** returning to the sections cited above at a later time.

Regardless of your level of experience in the creative problem-solving arena, we wish you success as you continue optimizing the magic of your mind.

bearly limited

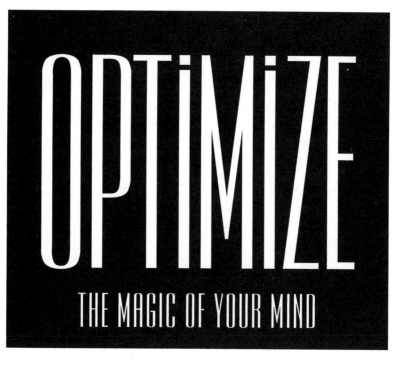

OPTIMIZE

THE MAGIC OF YOUR MIND

SIDNEY J. PARNES

IN ASSOCIATION WITH

The Creative Education Foundation, Inc.

BEARLY LIMITED · BUFFALO, NEW YORK

Copyrights & Permissions

Contents

Part I — Focus On The Beginner

Introduction To Part I: An Overview

Creative problem solving is not a mystery. It involves techniques that can be mastered and applied on a daily basis.

Why Continuously Strengthen Our Creative Abilities?

Learn to spot more opportunities — to better deal with change — to create more options and make wise choices.

The Creative Thought-Process:
Can We See More And More Than Meets The Eye?

Create ideas and solutions by a blend of imagination and judgment, sprinkled with humor and optimism.

Part II — Focus On The Practitioner

All royalties from this book are assigned to The Creative Education Foundation, Inc. to perpetuate Alex F. Osborn's work of encouraging more creative growth and achievement in all endeavors.

About The Authors
& Contributors

Sidney J. Parnes, Ph.D., is Professor Emeritus of Creative Studies at the State University College at Buffalo (SUCB). In 1955 he attended his first Creative Problem-Solving Institute (CPSI) in Buffalo with Alex F. Osborn, founder of the Creative Education Foundation, as his mentor. In the years that followed, Osborn and Parnes refined the five step divergent/convergent approach to Creative Problem-Solving while at the State University of New York at Buffalo (SUNY).

In 1967, Parnes moved to SUCB where he ultimately established the Interdisciplinary Center for Creative Studies and then in 1975, the first Master's Degree Program in Creative Studies in the United States.

Dr. Parnes also served as President of The Creative Education Foundation, Inc. from 1967 to 1984. He is a recipient of many national and international honors.

Among his many writings are: **Source Book For Creative Problem-Solving: A Fifty Year Digest Of Proven Innovation Processes; Visionizing;** and **Creative Behavior Guidebook.** He co-authored: **Guide To Creative Action; Creative Actionbook;** and **Toward Supersanity, Channeled Freedom.** His credits also include numerous magazine and journal articles. (See pages 166-168 of Annotated References.)

Worth Loomis, M.B.A., served as President of The Hartford Graduate Center (an affiliate of Rensselaer Polytechnic Institute) in Hartford, Connecticut, and also serves as Chairman of Life Technologies, Inc.

(Gaithersburg, MD) and COLT's Manufacturing (Hartford). He came to HGC in 1989 from a distinguished career in multinational manufacturing, including President of the Dexter Corporation from 1975-88.

Prior to joining the Dexter Corporation, Mr. Loomis was with the Medusa Corporation (Cleveland), Clevite Corporation (Cleveland), International Research & Development Corporation (Istanbul), and Reynolds & Company (New York City). He graduated as an industrial engineer from Yale University and earned his M.B.A. in international finance at New York University.

He is presently Visiting Professor of Faith and Public Life at The Hartford Seminary.

Photography by Deborah Boardman Photography

Robert A. Partridge, M.D., is an internationally-known author, researcher, teacher, and a consultant in creative thinking, mental training, intra- and interpersonal skills. He teaches creative problem-solving skills in his practices of psychiatry, peak performance athletics, and wellness. Throughout his life, he has focused on the interconnectedness of mind, body, and spirit and its holistic relationship to the health of both the individual and society.

In 1993, he published **Peak Performance Squash And Tennis!** and now serves as Special Consultant in Sports Psychiatry, Mental Training and Health to the International Professional and United States Squash Racquets Associations. Chair of Wellness Education, Training and Research at Drexel University since 1988, he recently combined his knowledge and experience in wellness and creative problem solving into the book titled **Take Charge Of Your Family's Health.**

Foreword

What you are holding in your hand is the greatest favor Sid Parnes could have done for readers: he has pulled together everything people need to know about Creative Problem Solving (CPS). Used for the past half century by businesses, universities, and individuals, CPS is a process that has improved the status quo and helped resolve conflict in the most efficient manner possible.

Is CPS a mystery? Not really. The techniques are well-known and have withstood the test of time. However, these techniques, like any other skill used in day-to-day life, must be learned. Starting with Chapter One, you can begin to teach yourself the fundamentals of CPS. If you are past the beginner stage, augment your skills with the guided exercises in Part II, starting with Chapter Seven, and for instructors and leaders, Part III, starting with Chapter Thirteen provides guidelines for facilitating groups or mentoring individuals.

I remember the first time I formally participated in the Creative Problem Solving process. The top three Research and Development people from each of our eight divisions of the Dexter Corporation assembled for a two-day conference on improving R & D productivity. (The Dexter Corporation's annual expenditures in this field ranked among the top Fortune 100 companies, and therefore merited special attention.) We used two facilitators from a research university, and at the end of the first day of the conference, we had created a list of procedure modifications that all participants enthusiastically supported. We not only liked our list, but we liked each other, and I still remember the gathering as one of our best meetings. From then on, I was a confirmed believer in CPS.

I have now moved from a business setting to an academic one, and these techniques are equally applicable here. Using Creative Problem Solving, various aspects of university life — from our mission statement, to a morale problem, to determining critical success factors,

By Worth Loomis

to the changing role of our libraries — have been explored. CPS was also used to examine the application of Total Quality Management to an educational institution, and its future applications seem limitless. In other words, anything new or difficult or important that needs to be accomplished can be done through Creative Problem Solving.

There was a time when only the leader or manager of a group was looked to for new ideas and answers to roadblocks. But the pace of change has quickened and society's global problems have become more complex. New frameworks are needed to address modern-day concerns, and the innovative and creative answers that organizations require can only be developed by people with Creative Problem-Solving skills throughout the organization.

Sid Parnes has spent fifty years facilitating widely diverse groups in problem-solving situations and he believes that the best way to release creative juices is to energize the CPS process with fun and laughter. Throughout his extensive experience in CPS coursework, institutes and workshops, he has developed and refined the ideas presented within this volume. This book is a marvelous combination of nuts and bolts knowledge with a sure grasp of the underlying theory, all wrapped up in an easy-to-read and humorous presentation.

Reader, enjoy the journey that lies ahead of you.

Prologue

The Heart Of The Book

This book is meant to be a hands-on opportunity for you to experience and practice the creative problem-solving (CPS) process until it becomes a comfortable way of extending your creative abilities to all of your activities. Part I gives you an experiential introduction. Part II extends this to your intensive application of the CPS process to a variety of your goals, desires, challenges, and concerns. Part III helps you be more effective as a facilitator/leader/mentor of CPS; it provides detailed suggestions for facilitating others — students, friends, family, colleagues, mentees, employees, children, etc. through each step of CPS. The suggestions can also be of help to individuals wishing to become more effective in their own use of the process. Preceding the detailed suggestions in Part III, I have included a short chapter on my interpretation of the nature and qualities of an effective facilitator. In the closing brief chapters, I present some of my recent thinking, including an "ing" philosophy of CPS.

Re The Foreword:

In the Foreword, Worth Loomis cites concise, diverse examples of the use and value of Creative Problem Solving (CPS) in his positions as President of a Fortune 100 company and then as President of a graduate academic institution. An industrial engineer with a master's degree in business, he provides a broad range of effective applications of the CPS process. From his first-hand experience, Loomis explains how to use this book, both for beginners and for readers who are advanced in CPS processes. He also makes clear to all users of this "hands-on" book the importance in today's world of increasing one's skills in CPS.

Re The Reflections:

I wrote this introductory piece especially for practitioners and facilitator-leaders of CPS. They will undoubtedly want to read it first. In it I deal with such matters as the extensive, substantiating research under-pinning CPS, the "creative stance", styles of creativity, new insights into process and technique, future efforts I plan to undertake, the educational revolution I foresee, and my two most important publications for further study. If you are beginning your work in CPS, you may want to read the Reflections after you have experienced more, especially in Parts One and Two.

Re The Epilogue:

The Epilogue by Psychiatrist Robert Partridge introduces research information re the creatively functioning individual, as well as state-of-the-art information on the human brain and the new theories that research data suggest. This will probably prove to be extremely encouraging to readers of this book. Some of you who are anxious to understand more of the theoretical aspects surrounding the subject of creativity may even prefer to digest the Epilogue before embarking on the practical applications starting in Chapter One. Those who prefer to dive right into the exercises provided in Parts One or Two, do go right ahead; but remember to reinforce your experiences by reading the Epilogue later, perhaps even before you start to apply more from Part Three.

Re The Annotated References:

See these for a brief introduction to my key publications that contain very detailed information, including research data, theoretical background, and extensive course material for advanced study; also for brief introductions to Osborn's four classic books on the subject.

The Book's Derivations

The Osborn/Parnes CPS process has had a half-century of intense research and development, and application by individuals and groups in the widest variety of fields and professions as well as in their personal lives. They ranged from business people to educators and government personnel, scientists to artists, military officers to church groups, mentally challenged to gifted students, high school students to Ph.D.'s in all disciplines. This book is based on my own 50 years of facilitating such groups through CPS, including over 40 years of applying and refining the creative approaches introduced to education, industry, and government by Alex F. Osborn in the 1940s and 1950s. I had the privilege of working with him personally during the last 10 years of his life. All royalties from this book are assigned to the Creative Education Foundation to help perpetuate Osborn's work of encouraging more creative growth and achievement in all endeavors.

The concepts embodied in this book have developed as a result of my years of association with hundreds of leaders in the field of creative studies and creative problem-solving. It would be impractical to identify the countless ideas that germinated from sessions or conversations with these leaders, who serve as the faculty for the Creative Problem-Solving Institutes sponsored by the Creative Education Foundation in Buffalo and around the nation. I owe them my profound thanks for their contributions and stimulation. I have, of course, acknowledged specific references but have kept them to a very minimum because of the nature of this book.

Two of these leaders became full-time colleagues whose constant contributions were incalculable during our close association for the majority of my years in Buffalo: Angelo M. Biondi and Ruth B. Noller. To them I am deeply indebted.

The material presented has been greatly enriched by feedback from well over 100,000 participants in institutes, courses, workshops, and experiential sessions that I have conducted. We research each offering for continual refinement and development of our processes. Hence I wish to express my sincere gratitude for the participation of all those involved in this "living laboratory."

In addition to Osborn, the other individual who has made the most significant and indelible contribution to this book is Beatrice F. Parnes, my wife and professional associate, who has been my best sounding board for my ideas, and with whom I have had the pleasure of living and working for the past 50 years.

Reflections

During the fifteen years since the publication of *The Magic of Your Mind* (Parnes, 1981) and the eleven years since writing *A Facilitating Style of Leadership* (Parnes, 1985), I have been extensively refining and extending Alex Osborn's Creative Problem-Solving (CPS) method- ologies. This revision and combining of those two books is one result.

Substantiating Research*

While Osborn was writing in the early '40s and '50s, there was no scientific substantiation of his ideas — only his own firm convictions based on his personal lifetime experience and his work in guiding executives in his advertising agency. Since then, hundreds of scientific studies have confirmed Osborn's strong convictions. More than a dozen of them have shown evidence of gains by experimental subjects in their ability to solve *real-life* problems more effectively after a course in CPS principles and procedures. The real-life criteria involve areas of academic accomplishment, personal adjustment, and industrial problem solving.

By the mid-1980s, the U.S. literature contained five major sum- maries showing significant positive results of deliberate attempts to nurture creative abilities across the disciplines. The largest single sum- mary, by E. Paul Torrance, covers 142 individual research investigations on nurturing creative ability. Within that compilation are 22 evaluating the specific model used in CPS; 20 of these showed significant positive effects. In 1985 Dr. Torrance reported at a creativity symposium that he had uncovered 500 additional studies since the 142 mentioned above, a dozen years earlier, with approximately the same pattern of

---

*For details on the research studies mentioned in these "Reflections," see Parnes, S. J., "The Creative Studies Project", and Kirton, M. J., "Adaptors and Innovators; Cognitive Style and Personality." In Isaksen, S. G. (Ed.), *Frontiers in Creativity Research: Beyond the Basics*. Buffalo, NY: Bearly Limited, 1987.

results. While limitations and deficiencies of studies are frequently pointed out by reviewers, the general conclusions are the same: Creative abilities can be developed by deliberate programs and methods.

Your Creative Stance

As you experience more and more of the activities provided through this current book, I anticipate you will move closer and closer to achieving what I call a "creative stance" in life — where you have internalized the CPS process so fully that your behavior manifests it continually in all your actions and reactions.

When Osborn published his first book, *How To Think Up,* a half-century ago, and his other publications over the next two decades, people tended to apply his processes only occasionally in their own particular fields—especially in business and industry—but not as much in their lives in general. But some stuck with it, applying it over and over again on different challenges and problems as they did in Osborn's advertising firm. Osborn and others began to notice personality changes — for example, toward a more open, accepting, positive attitude toward ideas of their own or others. This is what I mean by a "creative attitude or stance," or by the term, "internalizing the process." These people tended to develop what Abraham Maslow called the "self-actualizing" individuals. They create new options in their lives, seeing things in new ways. They also understand and use what Carl Rogers called an "internal locus of evaluation" — relying on their own ability to judge and evaluate rather than relying only on others' judgments. When we bring together hundreds of people with the "creative stance" as at one of the Creative Education Foundation's annual institutes (CPSI), it provides an unbeatable atmosphere for creative learning and creative achieving.

Theoretical Roots

The pioneering creativity theorists like Abraham Maslow, Carl Rogers, J. P. Guilford, Donald MacKinnon, Frank Barron, Morris Stein, and Victor Lowenfeld provided deep roots for the subject of creativity. Together with other giants like J. W. Getzels, E. Paul Torrance, Calvin Taylor, and Joseph McPherson they provided not only the needed roots but also fundamental applications of creative process in education, business, industry, government — in all of the arts and sciences. My work at the Buffalo campuses of State University of New York capitalized on all these foundations.

Styles Of Creativity

In the last few decades, a body of research has emerged on "styles of creativity." Probably the most familiar is the work of Michael Kirton with his Adaptation Innovation theory. Kirton's assessment instrument rates people as adaptive creators or innovative creators. People tend to fall along a continuum between strongly adapting (make many improvements) and strongly innovative (make many breakthroughs). Knowledge of the style preferences of individuals is helpful in forming the best mix for group creative endeavors as well as for helping individuals understand and learn from each other when working in groups.

The CPS processes are designed to help any individual grow in both the adaptive and innovative directions — really to balance the two strengths as they are needed in any particular circumstance. Sometimes in trying to draw the line between a *major* adaptation and a *minor* innovation, I say to myself that perhaps God or Nature was the only true innovator. In that sense, the universe of created beings are all really adaptors. That seems to make the distinction clearer to me.

Process Refinements Never End!

During a recent CPSI while this book was in press, I awakened one morning with an important new insight regarding the evaluation criteria used in the CPS process. I felt it was important enough to change my plans for conducting a session I was scheduled to present that day. It made a most helpful difference! So I prepared the following paragraphs to insert in the proofs of this article in this book.

The early processes in my book, *Visionizing* (Parnes, 1988), emphasize the part of CPS known as "mess or objective-finding" and the quality of "sensitivity to problems." I might now term it "focusing on desires." It is what George Land refers to as "future pull." This sets the "pull," the desire, the goal, the vision. Then, after examining, with heightened awareness, existing elements of the situation in "Fact-Finding," we imagine expansively in "Problem-Finding" many conceivable directions or approaches which we call "In What Ways Might We" ("IWWMW") or "How To's" to attain the desires (visions). We then use our imagination extensively in transforming, combining, synthesizing elements of the situation into many, many ideas that may conceivably help reach in the direction of the vision, desire, goal.

Then in my current way of best handling the process, I make a *crude, rough plan* out of the best ideas I can synthesize into a potential solution — a way of reaching toward the goal, vision, desire. I use intuition, hunches, "gut-level" feelings in addition to all logical bases I have for making judgments as I choose ideas to weave into my plan, the way an artist might construct a mosaic of the elements at hand. This brings me to convergence at the end of the "Idea-Finding" step.

As I move now into "Solution-Finding," instead of generating the longest list of *criteria* with which to evaluate my plan — a procedure which many people find difficult or confusing — I now bring about greater *awareness* of criteria and their *constructive* usefulness by applying Guilford's "improvements of common objects or situations" test. By this test, what was Guilford measuring? The quality of "sensitivity to problems." What is sensitivity to problems other than the ability to recognize *criteria* where an object or situation falls short, is deficient. Realization of this, therefore, provides an *opportunity* for improvement. If I can make it better, I am obviously aware, consciously or subconsciously, of criteria on which it was deficient.

Therefore, when I ask people to list many improvements for a rough plan, they are able to do so without confusion — and they immediately see the benefit of their heightened sensitivity or awareness in refining the plan for greater acceptance. If I wish to stretch this process more deeply, I probe with the specific list of improvement-questions listed on page 137.

With the above "forward-thrust" in "Solution-Finding," — getting immediately into ideas for greater acceptance — we have actually moved directly into "Acceptance-Finding" — without formal criteria lists, evaluation grids, etc. In this final step, we then search for ideas for "sanding, polishing, and packaging" the improved plan into its final form for presentation. Many times, however, fundamental reconstruction ideas are discovered as well, and the plan is changed accordingly.

As to the "30 Questions" checklist in "Acceptance-Finding," (see page 139), I had often used this list as a replacement for both "Solution-Finding" and "Acceptance-Finding" after I had had participants develop a "gut-level" crude plan from all the ideas they had conceived through "Idea-Finding." It provides a set of questions that elicit sensitivity and resulting improvements, in a somewhat redundant *but not repetitive* way as do the questions mentioned on page 137.

Finke's "Pre-inventive Forms"

Just before completing this expanded revision, I came in contact with a fascinating new body of research. It is reported in Ronald Finke's

book, *Creative Imagery,* subtitled, "Discoveries and Inventions in Visualization"[1]*. The research encourages strongly the imagery processes applied in my recent books. It shows impressive evidence of the universality and effectiveness of the ability to image. Finke applies an exercise that I feel will be invaluable in strengthening anyone's effectiveness at using imagery in CPS.

The exercise, for which impressive research data are presented, involves using imagery to conceive and develop "pre-inventive forms" in the invention process. For example, one set of parts the author provides from which to develop "pre-inventive forms" is: cube, wheels, cone. You are to close your eyes and imaginatively play with the three parts, not to create in your imagination a *known* object but instead an *interesting* shape; then find a useful application of some kind for it. This exercise is really parallel to many verbally-oriented exercises we use in CPS. For example, "forcing a relationship" between objects, or finding a way to turn a silly idea into a useful one.

The first time I myself tried this, I obtained an image of the cube balanced on a set of wheels attached across the middle of the bottom of the cube with a cone centered on the four corners of the top of the cube. I then thought of the following application: If a load of sand were placed inside such a cube-shaped container and a marker placed above the "balanced" point of the tip of the cone, the contents could be shifted gradually until the point stayed at the exact mark, which would indicate the load was completely balanced. Perhaps this would be useful for evenly balancing a load mounted on two wheels. This may or may not have any potential value as an invention — or it may already exist in some application — but it did provide me with my own small "aha" as I reflected for less than a minute on the challenge. I have now had the opportunity to introduce the exercise into workshops that I have conducted, with effective results.

The pre-inventive form I conceived serves actually as what Finke calls a "visual metaphor." The author's research shows that the vast majority of college subjects could do what I did within a minute's time, with no training! The brevity of the exercise seems to me to be one of its strongest powers. If participants applied deferred judgment and created *many* pre-inventive forms, and deferred again for *many* possible applications, the resultant invention might be more impressive and participants should tend to improve with extensive practice as in other skills developed in CPS.

---

* Footnotes appear at end of book.

After subjects incubated on the pre-inventive form, beyond the time limit, new meanings or possibilities would emerge in Finke's research. The author also discusses the effects of using category checklists to trigger the inventions — for example, architecture, physics and astronomy, biology, medicine, psychology, literature, music, political science. This is one such checklist he used. These category-lists could be the "Worlds" of Synectics for those familiar with that process. For experienced facilitators of CPS, Finke's "Pre-inventive Forms" exercise probably suggests many possible variations and adaptations, some of which he mentions in his book. He tested various adaptations and provides much helpful data.

The results and conclusions from Finke's study provide more support for the usefulness of intuition in the CPS process, particularly in the problem-finding aspect.

Future Efforts

I will next embark on a new major effort: integrating these CPS principles and procedures within the self-healing processes that have been growing rapidly in the last several decades. I intend in that coming work to help individuals effectively apply CPS to self-healing technologies toward the goal of high-level wellness — not merely physical wellness, but psychological, sociological, political, and spiritual wellness as well — moving toward what Maslow meant by the self-actualizing person.

My next publication will set out to help people effectively mate CPS, with its expanding imagery emphasis, with current programs on self-healing. It will be designed to help people become "self-healers" in a physical sense, "self-therapists" in a psychological sense, "self-integraters" in a social sense, "self-governors" in a political sense, and "self-godlike" in a spiritual sense. CPS can help people move from institutional help toward self-help as John Naisbitt predicted will happen as one of his ten "Megatrends." It can help provide strong empowerment to individuals — not ignoring the possible help of medicine, psychology, etc., but adding significantly to that help by people's own strengths and resources, and by their recognition of their own responsibility to use them. I intend to operationalize ideas that Osborn expressed or implied, or that I inferred from comments he made during the innumerable lengthy discussions I was fortunate enough to have with him during the ten years before his death in 1966.

Related Publications

This current book becomes the best condensation of what I have to offer on using CPS. For my *most comprehensive* work on *using* CPS, especially for instructors or for students willing to do intensive self-study, see *Visionizing* (Parnes, 1988). For my most comprehensive *general* work on CPS and related processes — a kind of mini-encyclopedia on the subject — see *Source Book For Creative Problem-Solving* (Parnes, 1992)

Educational "Velvet Revolution"

I can't help thinking, in closing these reflections, that the above books provide research substantiated tools for an educational revolution of the non-violent type we witnessed in some Eastern European countries. Czechoslovakia's "Velvet Revolution," as it was called, made possible in 1990 the largest conference ever held in that country — one on innovation and management. At that conference, top government and industry officials spoke of another impending revolution — that of introducing democratic management into a market-driven economy. I couldn't help think then — as I reflected on what they had accomplished so quickly politically and the plans they were now outlining economically: isn't it time for just as profound a "velvet" revolution in education — to really introduce, *full-scale,* the integration of CPS within the curricula of every educational institution in the nation and then the world. A current example at the University level is the Wharton School's graduate business degree at the University of Pennsylvania. *Business Week* in its May 13, 1991 issue described the major overhaul there as "Wharton rewrites the book on B Schools." Two of five main goals are to foster creativity and innovation, and to promote real-world problem-solving.

It is frequently claimed that it takes 50 years for the findings of educational research to work their way into widespread educational practice. If this is accurate, the coming decades should demonstrate a mainstream application in all of our schools of what is now taking place only in our most innovative ones. With the increasing availability of books, materials, and programs, we may see revolutionary dissemination and application now not only in education, but business, industry, and government as well.

Reprinted by courtesy of Vision Enterprises, Inc.

CHAPTER ONE

Introduction To Part I:
An Overview

Sure you can solve problems; you've been doing it all your life. But would you be happier discovering more opportunities in your problems? . . . More options? . . . Would you like to uncover new ways of viewing problems? . . . Would you like to put more of your ideas to work? . . . Well, this book is meant to help you do just that. It focuses on ways to tune up your creative power much like athletes tune up their physical power.

Many athletes fine-tune themselves to such a state of physical fitness that they are able to set world records with their performances. Yet while you may not set any records by extending your mental limits and fitness, you surely can keep beating your own previous performances — life-long.

If you utilize the processes presented in this book to sense what your problems truly are and then to solve them, research indicates the strong probability that you will find better ways to lead your life . . . run an organization...serve in community, state, and national affairs...etc.

Are You An Opportunity-Maker?

Regardless of the way you answered the question or regardless of your mental potential, you can significantly improve your capacity to sense and meet your problems and challenges . . . "opportunity-making," if you will. Or to put it another way, you can increase your ability to reach your desires and goals.

The primary emphasis of this introductory chapter is to answer possible questions that might surface as you experience this rather unconventional book. By way of further description:

- Part I will involve you in an orientation to creative problem-solving, including some brief applications to relevant desires, challenges, and concerns in your life.
- Part II will put you completely in the driver's seat. You will begin to apply researched approaches to dealing more

Drawing by S. Gross; ©1978 The New Yorker Magazine, Inc.

speedily and effectively with the concerns, desires, and challenges that you face, until the processes feel comfortable and natural to you. You may discover more and more opportunities for creative achievement in any situation that you are dealing with, as well as new options for effective decisions and action plans regarding your ideas.

• Part III will provide the best help I can offer you as you begin to lead others through the processes.

Want To Move Faster?

If you feel comfortably familiar with creative problem-solving approaches, you may want to move directly to Part II or Part III. There it is hoped that you will gain through intense involvement, an increased understanding, speed, and effectiveness with these approaches. In Part II they are programmed to help you sense challenges and opportunities in your life and work, and to implement responsible plans for action utilizing the ideas and options you generate.

Even if you opt to move directly to Part II or Part III, you may want to return to Part I later if you become curious about some of the processes that you experience. The processes will usually take you somewhere worthwhile, but you may not understand exactly how or why you got there. Part I will assist you in gaining that understanding, thus facilitating your travels through Part II by introducing you to more of your creative power.

My greatest joy is in turning people on to more of their creative potential — whether they consider themselves to be at the high or low end of the mental ability spectrum, whether they be professionals or students, old or young, leaders or laypeople — and to see them enjoy the *intrinsic* rewards that their creativity offers them.

In this book we will be dealing with *ahas* (new insights) and *ha-has* (humor). During 40 years of research and development of creative productivity, I have been making serious, significant points about creative problem-solving through the use of humorous cartoons. As you reflect on each cartoon, you may find supporting and extending messages beyond the verbal ones on the pages of the book. Furthermore, research[2] has confirmed my belief that a "fun" atmosphere, that is, one that contains humor, tends to spawn creative ideas. Laughter can often result from playing with ideas rather than dealing with them only in a logical, analytical way. As you "play" with the cartoons, you may notice their impact on the processes that you apply to your challenges and problems.

What Is Half Of Eight?

In our formal education, teachers usually defined the problem for us and told us how to solve it. They then asked *us* for *the* answer.

Question: "What is half of eight?" Answer: "Four." But what if I were to say that half of eight is zero? Would you scoff, shrug, be puzzled, or what? Think about it for a moment . . .

If you happened to smile to yourself or "light up" inside just a little, it might have been because you experienced a bit of an *aha*. Perhaps it was a mild "eureka" similar in type, but not in intensity, to Sir Isaac Newton's *aha* in his classic interpretation of the law of gravity when the apple fell on his head. You may have seen "8" as a visual rather than a mathematical concept. Then half of "8" becomes "o" — the top or bottom half — or "zero."

Of course, you might see something entirely different depending on how you view or interpret "half of eight" in your mind. Jot down some responses of what else it might become as you "play" with alternative ways of viewing "half" of "eight." When you finish, compare them with the collection of sample responses which appear below*.

The typical *aha* experience results from new and relevant connections made among elements within our brain and/or perceptual field. A long-time misconception was that these occurrences could only happen by random accidents and that one simply had to wait and *let* them happen. However, research findings continually show that individuals can employ processes to help increase the *likelihood* or *probability* that these kinds of connections will take place.

Ahas vary in power all the way from a few volts to enough intensity to light up the world. The result of Newton's experience with the falling apple would qualify as a high voltage *aha;* he had been struggling with the problem of gravity for some time. It was a powerful insight for him.

While super high voltage *ahas* occur rather infrequently, we can experience the 5 and 10 volt variety daily as we strive for new and relevant associations. And, even these can be increased to the 25, 50, and 100 levels on the *aha* voltage meter.

---

*$ = 3; VHH = 5 or 8; VI||II = 6 or 2; ate = ^{1}; $\mathcal{8}$ = 7.

Can We Speed Up Our Brains?

We are continually attempting to unshackle the brain so that it can better perform its natural process of idea production. George Land, in his well-known book *Grow or Die,* compares this mental process to the natural process of biological mutations. The exciting difference, he points out, is that nature's "survival of the fittest" is a wasteful process where most of the mutations are lost. In the mental process, the countless variations (mutations) that we call "ideas" can be evaluated *in the mind.* Thus only the ones with the most potential can be selected *mentally* and *then* developed, rather than indiscriminately developing all of the ideas and then scrapping all but the best.

You might refer to what we will be doing as "speedthinking." Whereas in "speedreading" we learn to read faster with greater comprehension, in "speedthinking" we learn to associate thoughts faster with greater effectiveness.

Are You Exercising All Of Your Brain?

You may recognize from recent articles about the right and left hemispheres of the brain that cartoon stimulation is designed to appeal to the "right, more imaging side" of your brain while the printed word appeals to the "left, more verbal side." Wherever they actually reside, both functions of your brain will be strengthened through the mental *exercising* outlined in these pages. I hope to involve you by questioning you, by providing you with the cartoon images to reflect on, and mostly by offering direct experiences for your participation. Remember as Aldous Huxley said:

> Experience is not what happens to you; it is what you do with what happens to you.

For example, fold your arms in front of you. Now separate them and fold them the *opposite* way. Did that feel strange or uncomfortable? Most people find that it does.

Incidentally, what happened doesn't seem to relate to left- or right-handedness — only to habit. It is often equally uncomfortable to change a mental habit or set. Thus a basic purpose of this book is to help you "break set" more easily and comfortably.

Growth results from actually *experiencing* and *practicing* the processes. As I was once told, you can read all you want to about Freud, but sooner or later you've got to go out with guys or gals! Thus this book is not offered for passive reading, but for *active involvement* and *practice* with the creative problem-solving processes.

Do You Want To Involve Others?

I hope that you will introduce the exercises that follow to family members, friends at social gatherings, and work or study groups — particularly utilizing Part II for working together on common interests, desires, concerns, and challenges. The blank "white" spaces provided always mean, *Respond! Capture your thoughts.* Write, draw, symbolize, imagine — any response will do! Group members can do this aloud and/or by sharing responses, thus cross-fertilizing one another's thoughts.

Whether alone or in group settings, the program you will be following is designed to stimulate greater interplay between your cranial hemispheres. The interactions between the imaginative, playful you (representing the so-called "right-brain") and the logical, serious, judgmental you (representing the so-called "left-brain") will be harnessed to increase the probability of better decision-making as you deal with your desires, problems, and challenges.

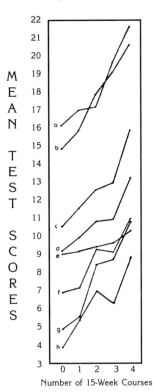

Number of 15-Week Courses

What Does The Research Show?

My 40 years of experience in nurturing creative ability in both normal and so-called "gifted" individuals has provided constant evidence of the "continuum of growth" concepts that I have stressed. Likewise, our formal research over that same period has provided supportive evidence.

Note the upward slope of the growth lines in the graph to the left. The base line refers to college students with five different levels of creative studies experience: no courses, one, two, three, and four semester-long courses. There is almost totally consistent growth on eight tests of different facets of creative ability as more and more creative problem-solving was experienced by the students.[3]

The references at the end of this book provide summaries of our research studies, as well as additional studies on the deliberate development of creative productivity.

"Foster here is the left side of my brain, and Mr. Hoagland is the right side of my brain."

Drawing by Lorenz; © 1977 The New Yorker Magazine, Inc.

One particular industrial study[4] showed two different levels of creative producers in a company suggestion-system *both* moved significantly up the continuum after a creative problem-solving course. The gains were reflected by an almost doubling of both the number and dollar amount of awards received. These results show not only an increased ability in *making suggestions,* but also in *gaining acceptance* for them as well.

EFFECT OF CREATIVE TRAINING ON AWARDS

Average of Low Producers

From ($33)   To   ($79)

Average of High Producers

From ($39)   To   ($83)

CHAPTER TWO

Why Continuously Strengthen Our Creative Abilities?

Let's start out with a brief "pretest." It, like a picture, may answer this question better than a thousand words.

1. Fill in the answer.
   A _____ of horses went by.
   a. *steam*   b. *team*   c. *stream*

2. How many squares do you see?

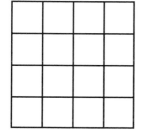

3. What questions might you ask about this configuration?

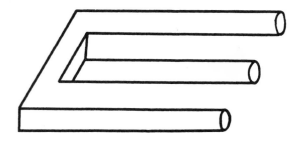

4. Think of a challenge in your life and how to meet it.

How Do Your Answers Measure Up?

What was your response to Question 1? If your formal education tended to provide you with a problem and the method for arriving at the solution, then you probably chose "team" as the response. That was the answer the teacher who designed the test expected to see.

On the other hand, you may have chosen "stream," as a great many people do, or "steam" as an occasional individual does. You may have created the mental image of a herd of horses "flowing" by, or of a group of horses with clouds of vapor billowing from their nostrils on a frigid day. How about imaging a few more possibilities that a "stream of horses" or "steam of horses" might suggest?

In your response to Question 2 you may have counted the entire square as well as the 16 smaller ones . . . Or you may have added the square formed by the inside four squares . . . Or the four quadrants (squares) formed by each corner set of four squares . . . or . . . ? Think about it some more . . .

Might you even visualize infinity as the answer?

One student did and he felt that I wasn't very imaginative because I had asked him to find only 30 different squares. He saw infinity as the answer by viewing the figure as a wall of blocks, infinitely deep, and imagining the infinite sets of squares in the mass of blocks.

Extreme *rigidity* with respect to the often-asked question "What is 2 and 2?" leads to the simple answer "4." Extreme *looseness* could lead to a highly unusual answer such as 897 — or any number that pops into one's head, with no relation to reality. But the happy compromise of enough "looseness" to allow flexibility, yet enough "tightness" to maintain reality, produces answers like "2 and 2 may be 4, 22, $\frac{2}{2}$, etc., depending on how you put the digits together."

Can you make four 9s equal 100?

How about 99 $\frac{9}{9}$? or . . . ?

Of course, these aren't the answers that most teachers expect and require as responses to conventional school problems. There we may have to conform to the rigid requirements. However, if we tune our imaginations to see questions in a variety of ways, we will often produce original ideas to meet problems and challenges successfully. And, our current economy requires solutions that can substitute greater innovation for reduced resources.

Can You See The 'Problems' In A Mess?

In the first two items, the questions were posed to you. Your response to the team-steam-stream question had to be selected from the three choices provided — hopefully the "right" one. In the 16-square item you were free to give whatever answer *your* definition and method arrived at. But, how often are you presented with the opportunity to make up the problems — raise the questions — yourself?

In the "3-pronged blivet" question, you did not have a problem, only a mess. You had to ask questions in order to formulate problems. What if the problem had been to *build* the "gismo" illustrated? Could you have done it? Think about it for a moment . . .

A group of engineers did just that. They used wire instead of inked lines and soldered the wires at all the same points where the lines were joined, producing a two-dimensional figure.

Yet another group of engineers insisted that it couldn't be made. When they saw the wire version, they argued that it was wrong because it was "two-dimensional!" The inventive group retorted, "Who said it was three-dimensional!" I had not placed such a constraint. Had you?

Now look at the loosely defined, "Think of a challenge in your life and how to meet it." In order to deal with it you must *become sensitive* to a mess, problem, challenge, or unmet desire. You then have the opportunity to use your own knowledge and imagination in approaching it and reaching your own decision. Isn't that what much of life is all about? In contrast, much that we learn in the way of specific knowledge to feed back on tests may become irrelevant as circumstances change.

For example, I once heard a professor of medicine say to his students at the conclusion of a course:

> Within five years, about one-half of what I have told you will either be untrue or not worth a darn. This doesn't really bother me; but what *does* irritate me is that I can't even tell you which half is which!

> After all, the atom was taught as irreducible — until World War II.

How Do We Cope With The Changing World?

The world is changing drastically — and quickly. Alvin Toffler, in his book *Future Shock,* dramatized the geometric changes we face:

> It has been observed, for example, that if the last 50,000 years of man's existence were divided into lifetimes of approximately 62 years each, there have been about 800 such lifetimes. Of these 800, fully 650 were spent in caves.
>
> Only during the last 70 lifetimes has it been possible to communicate effectively from one lifetime to another—as writing made it possible to do. Only during the last six lifetimes did masses of men ever see a printed word. Only during the last four has it been possible to measure time with any precision. Only in the last two has anyone anywhere used an electric motor. And the overwhelming majority of all the material goods we use in daily life today have been developed within the present, the 800th, lifetime.[5]

What changes will the 801st lifetime introduce? Can you foresee what knowledge you will need five or ten or twenty years from now to meet your life's problems?

Change seems not only inevitable, but necessary and important as new factors are introduced into our awareness. The question is: Do we constantly react to change or do we *introduce* and *control* it by *our* actions; can we *pro*-act rather than *react*? If all signs point to our future being overcome by pollution, yet we reverse the trend by turning pollution into an asset or otherwise creatively dealing with it, we may truly *shock the future* instead of suffering *future shock.*

We may not be sure what we'll need to *know* for the future, but we can be reasonably sure that we will need increasing ability to sense and meet the challenges and problems our changing lives present rather than using tranquilizers to deal with them.

Unfortunately, we sometimes are spoon-fed so much in our lives that we lose the urge to think. A personnel executive claimed that only 10 new junior executives out of 200 responded well to an opening assignment to "look around for a few months and then think of what you want to do." The remaining 190 found the situation too unstructured and insecure; they had no urge to think. The executive maintained: "We live in a wonderful age where we can get whatever we want; the problem is what we should want."

How well would you have performed on a final exam composed *entirely* of questions similar to "Think of a challenge in your life and how to meet it." Stretch your imagination on that question for a few more minutes. List some *new* challenges in *your* work and life, some "new things to want" — then choose one and list some ways that you can dream up to meet it.

College students and adults at the *end* of a creative studies course or institute respond quite well to tasks like the one you just tackled. I tried an experiment once by walking into an hour-and-a-quarter *opening session* of our course, handing out an exam booklet, and telling students to "Think of a problem and solve it." Then I simply sat through the entire period without saying anything. The students smiled, giggled, squirmed or doodled, but most of them did not produce anything very profound.

When the same "exam" was given and collected at the *final session* of the course, the students quickly asked, "We'll get these back, won't we?" They asked because they had recorded valuable ideas and plans in their booklets, not because they wanted to see how we "marked" them. Contrast this to the first-day experiment where none of the students asked to have the exam booklet returned because they didn't value their products then.

What happened between the first and last sessions described above is the emphasis of this book. If you did extremely well on the previous pages, you might want to merely skim the rest of Part I and move right into Part II as suggested earlier.

Are You Boxed In Mentally In Your Decisions?

Our decisions are affected by the way we view and define our problems and challenges. How boxed in are you? . . . Are you using all the space you have? . . . Do you bulge out the sides occasionally? . . . Or step out once in a while? . . . Or even move to a bigger box?

Can You Create More Options?

Too many of our decisions are habit-bound, straight-jacketed by imaginary boxes. Jot down a few "either-or" decisions that you are currently facing. They can range from the complex (i.e., Should I keep my job *or* go for advanced training? Should I fire him/her *or* not?) to the less demanding (i.e., Should I go to the movie tonight *or* not?).

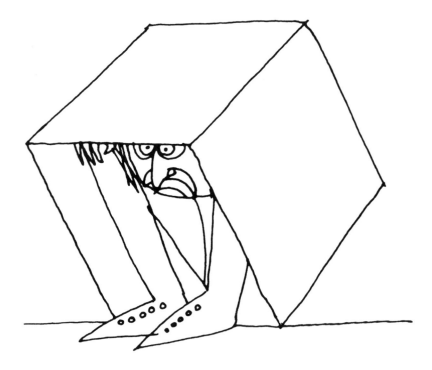

Reprinted by courtesy of Vision Enterprises, Inc.

Because neither of our two alternatives is fully acceptable, we may find either decision painful or unsatisfactory. Too often we merely examine what exists, choose the least of available evils, and act accordingly.

Publisher Charles Scribner, Jr. provided a striking illustration of how to break past painful "either-or" decisions by creating a new alternative:

> Marjorie Kinnan Rawlings had written a children's book called *The Secret River,* which we decided to publish in 1955, two years after her death. Set in the South, it was about a little girl whose mother was a hairdresser. It was not made clear whether the girl was supposed to be black or white, and we were a little troubled by this ambiguity. Whatever our decision, we could land on the wrong side of the school boards. Then I had an inspiration. I had the entire book printed in black ink on brown paper, so there was no imputed color in the illustrations. That was one of my silent contributions to dissolving the color barrier in the 1950s[6].

How can you know what you *should* do until you know all that you *might* do? President Kennedy had his own commentary on the "either-or" type of decision-making. He asserted, "We refuse to be limited to the two alternatives of all-out nuclear war or total humiliation."

When you make *creative* decisions, you avoid putting yourself in the "either-or" box by: first, speculating on what "might be" from a variety of viewpoints; then sensing and anticipating all conceivable consequences or repercussions of the variety of actions contemplated; finally choosing and developing the best alternative — in full awareness.

Redefine one of the problems you listed, focusing on what you are really trying to accomplish. For example,

"Should I paint this room or shouldn't I?" might become, "How might I make this room more attractive?" or "How might I save money in redecorating this room?" "Should I fire him/her or not," could be restated as "How might I get this employee to work effectively?" or even "How might I get this job done effectively?" Each broader definition allows us to create a greater panorama of possibilities from which to deliberately choose.

After thinking up many ideas for these new problem definitions, we may still decide to *paint* the room or *fire* the employee. But now it will be a deliberate choice from among many existing alternatives, not a blind, habit-bound, "Yes, it's dirty so I will paint it" or "No, it's not so dirty, so I won't" — "Yes, he's impossible, so I'll fire him" or "No, he's not that bad, so I won't."

Paul MacCready, President of Aero Vironment, Inc., related this account of the way we unnecessarily constrain ourselves by our problem definitions:

> I was discussing, with a 10-year-old, how you put a needle on water and have the surface tension keep it afloat. The question was, "how to set on the water the largest possible needle which could stay afloat." How would you lower it and release it delicately? With your fingers? With tiny wire hooks? With an electro-magnet? After a little discussion, the 10-year-old said, "freeze the water, set the needle on it, and let the water melt." Would that really work? I suspect so . . . the question was "how do you get the largest possible needle to be floating on the water," not "how do you set it down." I had introduced an unnecessary constraint.

Are You Making Deliberate Choices?

We can travel to Europe by sailboat, steamboat, plane, or perhaps even by rocket. If for some reason or other, we decide to go by sailboat, we do so with the realization that the other means of travel are also available. This represents deliberate choice from among a variety of alternatives as contrasted to "blind" acceptance.

To do nothing, when there is an opportunity to take action, could also be an alternative decision. On the other hand, we often avoid taking action because we have not uncovered the variety of alternative approaches that might be available to us.

So, try defining another one of those "either-or" dilemmas you listed earlier in a different way. Instead of, "should I do 'this' or 'that,' " ask yourself . . . "What do I really want to accomplish? What would I really like to have happen?" Then rephrase the problem in a couple of new ways and see if it allows you some new latitude for creating alternatives. See if it gets you out of your mental box. I hope you may see the problem in ways beyond that in which you originally expressed it.

CHAPTER THREE

The Creative Thought-Process: Can We See More And More Than Meets The Eye?

We have increased the average lifespan significantly by current health measures. In a physical sense we are coming to know increasing *wellness* as our goal rather than merely freedom from illness. But, can we extend the span of our *mental* lifetime even more dramatically? In a mental sense can we learn to progress along a perhaps infinite continuum of greater wellness and mental agility? Can we learn to tap our full potential?

Mark Twain told of a visitor to heaven who asked St. Peter if he might meet the greatest general who had ever lived. St. Peter responded by pointing out a nearby inhabitant. The visitor protested that he had known *that* man, who was not a general but only a cobbler. "Oh yes," replied St. Peter, "but if he had been a general he would have been the greatest of them all."

How about *your* potential? Let's look at a fundamental aspect of it — your *imagination*. How has it fared with you in childhood? . . . As an adult? How does it function in your problem solving and decision making? How does it affect the fulfillment of your creative potential?

Are You In A Cultural Cocoon?

We begin life in the shelter of a mother's womb, much like life in a cocoon. Then we break out. And the child we become is a butterfly full of imagination.

But what happened to you after that? Have you returned to a cocoon? . . . A psychological cocoon? . . . A cultural cocoon? . . . Are you now in what Ashley Montagu once quipped, "a womb with a view"?

Ironically, the child has oodles of imagination, but often very little judgment; the adult acquires oodles of judgment, but often loses the imagination.

Use your imagination to image the following: a very strange looking animal riding in a funny looking wagon. Then see how it compares with images on the next page.

© King Features Syndicate.
Reprinted with special permission of
King Features Syndicate.

Our objective, therefore, is to allow knowledge to grow without stifling the natural associative streams of the mind that can lead us into valuable inventive directions. This involves imagination that is not only *developed* but *disciplined* as well.

By way of example, fourth grader Clint Lenz made news when he won a $1,000 prize and one week in Washington for his invention, a glow-in-the-dark toilet seat. The toilet will go into the Smithsonian and several plastic companies are interested in purchasing the idea. Ironically, the youngster's family has a number of professional plumbers among its membership; none of them thought up the idea.

Are You An Adult Child?

"Adult children" strike an effective balance between imagination and judgment as they meet challenges and opportunities that many others aren't even aware of. They see things in ways other than originally presented; their minds produce interesting new associations, not stale playbacks. They make new and relevant responses to challenges or problems that are both explicit and implicit in their lives. Would you describe yourself as an "adult child"?

What's Funny About Creativity?

We all seem to enjoy fun and humor but we tend to limit our involvement with it to recreation or entertainment. Yet creativity and humor are closely related, both frequently relying on *appropriate absurdity*. Humor, considered as *appropriate absurdity,* contains the same "opposing" elements found in most descriptions of creative behavior; i.e., the mating of playfulness and seriousness, of fantasy and reality, of nonsense and purpose, of irrational and rational.

For example, take the poetic expression "a lion's ferocious chrysanthemum head." Chrysanthemum as used here is "irrationally apropos," an appropriate absurdity.

The humorist or cartoonist often presents a situation that can be viewed in two ways, or sets up an expectation which is reversed or contradicted in a surprising way. It is the sudden "getting" of the second, unexpected relationship or viewpoint, or seeing the surprising con-tradiction, that makes the situation funny. No one tells you what to look for. (A joke falls flat if someone has to tell you what's funny — if you don't "get" it.) The humorist presents the story so cleverly that you almost automatically generate another way, beyond the obvious one, of interconnecting the data presented — absurdly perhaps, but yet appropriate. It surprises and delights you, probably resulting in laughter.

A humorist once observed that the name of the well-known advertising agency of Batten, Barton, Durstine & Osborn sounded like a trunk falling down the stairs. This may seem merely *absurd* until you say the agency's name out loud and see how appropriate it is. He saw a relationship that was surprising, yet *appropriate* — an appropriate absurdity.

Most really new ideas sound funny because they involve a new and strange relationship among known facts, yet a relationship that has an element of meaning or reality to it. Thus both humor and creativity depend largely on our being able to see something in more than the obvious, expected way.

You might like to try your hand at creating humor yourself by seeing something in an unusual way. How about a few titles for the "drawing" shown below? Try listing at least one "appropriate absurdity."

You may have come up with *Ice-Skating Rink, Squiggles* or a number of perfectly appropriate titles. Perhaps you thought up some like, *Los Angeles Freeway at 5 P.M.* or *Circles Getting Dizzy,* which seem to combine appropriateness with absurdity.

Like appropriate absurdities, creative ideas often provide us with chuckles or *ha-has.* But more often they give us *ahas,* familiarly depicted as the glowing lightbulbs in cartoons.

Humor's appropriate absurdity becomes the *aha* of creative thought. It results from a *new* connection, association, or relationship that proves to be *relevant,* valuable, satisfying, or harmonious to you.

Try your hand at experiencing a visual *aha.* Is the airplane coming toward you or moving away from you?

Study it again. Can you make it switch direction at will? If you can't see the airplane coming toward you, imagine yourself looking *down* on it from above. If you can't see it flying away, imagine yourself *under* it watching it fly off to your left.

Chances are that when you first looked at the figure, you saw it moving in only one direction. Then, either quickly or after some concentration, you may have gained the other perception. At the very moment you experienced the new perception, especially if it took a while, you probably experienced a mild *aha* — a slight "thrill of discovery" of the new viewpoint.

In a metaphorical sense, the visual *aha* might represent any new insight we get, particularly when we suddenly recognize something positive in a situation that formerly looked totally negative. The problem magically turns into an opportunity.

Can You See The Positive In Anything?

The optimist, while aware that a glass of water is "half-empty," elects to focus on the "half-full" part; the pessimist views it only as "half-empty." Someone once viewed dirt as "basically matter in a wrong place." Imagination plays an important part in the way we see things.

Fran Stryker, originator of the Lone Ranger, commissioned two individuals to independently appraise a parcel of land that he was interested in purchasing. One reported, "There are dead trees all over the place. There's a stream so narrow that you can almost always step across it; and the weeds are six feet high." The second person, reporting on the *same* tract of land, commented that: "There is enough firewood on the land to last a lifetime, there's a stream wide enough in one spot to dam up into a swimming hole, and from the size of the weeds, it's the richest, most fertile land in the area." Fortunately Fran relied on the second report, and developed his delightful "Fiction Farm," complete with fireplace, swimming hole, and garden.

Even seemingly irrelevant or accidental happenings can be turned into positives that take on new meaning in relation to our goal. An example is the case of the person who was picking sticky burrs off his trousers, as most of us have done after walking through the woods. He became intrigued with the way the burrs attached themselves to his clothing, and suddenly the idea behind the 'Velcro' fastener was born.

Inventor Charles Kettering pointed out that the average person obliterates 90% of the *good* in an idea because of the 10% *bad* that seems to be apparent. Opportunity-makers do just the opposite! They focus on what is *good* and develop it into something great. Their accomplishments are often met with sighs of "Why didn't I think of that?" when observed by others.

What it boils down to is that in behaving creatively, we continually search for positive implications of that which is already known or observable. What we call "luck" is often this knack of sensing or becoming aware of an opportunity or new meaning in a situation.

For example, a manufacturer of toilet tissue is reported to have discovered a carload of paper that failed to meet specifications. It was too thick and heavy to be made into the company's product. The unsatisfactory lot provided some new insights, and paper towels were born.

In another instance, a batch of soap was accidentally blended too long. The resultant mix had microscopic air bubbles throughout it. Seeing new implications in the accident, the manufacturer launched the famous advertising campaign for Ivory Soap — "It floats."

Sometimes in the hand-weaving of an Oriental rug, a mistake is made in the pattern; but the rug is not discarded. Rather, wisdom and imagination are combined to incorporate the mistake into an entirely new pattern, often more beautiful than the original.

Recognizing the possibility of *capitalizing* on the mistake might be the *luck* factor mentioned above. But, incorporating the new insight into the more beautiful pattern requires effort and persistence.

Luck doesn't generate the solution; *work* does! In the examples above of paper towels and the soap, it required much effort to implement the "lucky" insights into profitable products.

How About Some Low Voltage 'Ahas'?

Let's practice experiencing low voltage *ahas* by viewing some interesting pictures in more than one way — by seeing more than immediately meets the eye. In each picture you will undoubtedly see something "at first glance". Then go beyond the first perception, and see what else you might discover by viewing it from different perspectives, shifting figure and ground, etc.

You may find it difficult to make a new connection in some pictures. My purpose is not to frustrate you, but rather to expose you to stimuli of varying difficulty-levels, so that they might trigger *ahas* of different intensities. Play with the stimuli and have fun trying to reach new perceptions until you experience at least one *aha.*

Reprinted from *Handbook of Early Advertising Art*
by Clarence Hornung. © 1956, Dover Publications.

Reprinted with permission from the Creative Education Foundation, Inc.
Copyright© 1976.

'— And That Goverment of the People'

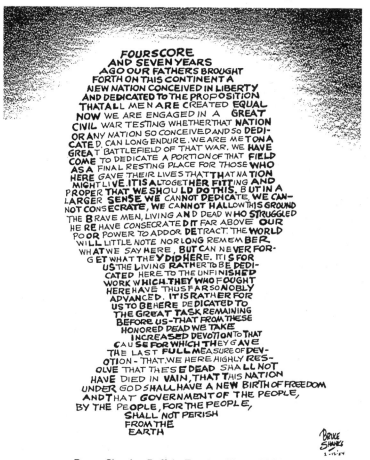

FOURSCORE
AND SEVEN YEARS
AGO OUR FATHERS BROUGHT
FORTH ON THIS CONTINENT A
NEW NATION CONCEIVED IN LIBERTY
AND DEDICATED TO THE PROPOSITION
THAT ALL MEN ARE CREATED EQUAL
NOW WE ARE ENGAGED IN A GREAT
CIVIL WAR TESTING WHETHER THAT NATION
OR ANY NATION SO CONCEIVED AND SO DEDI-
CATE D. CAN LONG ENDURE. WE ARE MET ON A
GREAT BATTLEFIELD OF THAT WAR. WE HAVE
COME TO DEDICATE A PORTION OF THAT FIELD
AS A FINAL RESTING PLACE FOR THOSE WHO
HERE GAVE THEIR LIVES THAT THAT NA TION
MIGHT LIVE. IT IS ALTOGETHER FITTING AND
PROPER THAT WE SHOULD DO THIS. BUT IN A
LARGER SENSE WE CANNOT DEDICATE, WE CAN-
NOT CONSECRATE, WE CANNOT HALLOW THIS GROUND
THE BRAVE MEN, LIVING AND DEAD WHO STRUGGLED
HE RE HAVE CONSECRATE D IT FAR ABOVE OUR
POOR POWER TO ADD OR DETRACT. THE WORLD
WILL LITTLE NOTE NOR LONG REMEMBER
WHAT WE SAY HERE, BUT CAN NEVER FOR-
GET WHAT THEY DID HERE. IT IS FOR
US THE LIVING RATHER TO BE DEDI-
CATED HERE TO THE UNFINISHED
WORK WHICH. THEY WHO FOUGHT
HERE HAVE THUS FAR SO NOBLY
ADVANCED. IT IS RATHER FOR
US TO BE HERE DEDICATED TO
THE GREAT TASK REMAINING
BEFORE US-THAT FROM THESE
HONORED DEAD WE TAKE
INCREASED DEVOTION TO THAT
CAUSE FOR WHICH THEY GAVE
THE LAST FULL MEASURE OF DEV-
OTION - THAT WE HERE HIGHLY RES-
OLVE THAT THESE DEAD SHALL NOT
HAVE DIED IN VAIN, THAT THIS NATION
UNDER GOD SHALL HAVE A NEW BIRTH OF FREEDOM
AND THAT GOVERNMENT OF THE PEOPLE,
BY THE PEOPLE, FOR THE PEOPLE,
SHALL NOT PERISH
FROM THE
EARTH

Bruce Shanks, Buffalo Evening News, 1964.

I hope you experienced a few *ahas* while playing with the pictures. If you didn't, prop up the pages on your dresser or desk and glance at them occasionally. See if anything new jumps out at you. Or look at the pictures with someone else, and give each other clues as to how to see them differently.

Your ability to see a person, an object or a situation in new ways pertains to all aspects of creative problem-solving. More opportunities to practice will be provided in later chapters.

What's Impossible?

Once we learn that everything can be viewed in many different ways, we may discover more of the positives inherent in any situation that we face. Furthermore, we may come to realize that the "impossible" is no longer absolute. Failures previously viewed as discouragements can become stepping stones to success.

Thomas Edison was known as a tireless opportunity-maker. After thousands of unsuccessful experiments on one of his projects, a discouraged assistant complained that they had achieved no results. "No results!", exclaimed Edison, "We've had wonderful results! We already know thousands of things that won't work."

A group of "opportunity-maker" chemists took on the challenge of making a "silk" purse from 100 pounds of sows' ears. They converted the gristle and skin to glue. Then they extruded it and dyed it, producing colored thread. On a small hand loom, they wove the silky thread into cloth and made a tasseled pocketbook. They proved their point: anything can be done.

Alan Mogensen, in his methods improvement program, reminds us that "the bumble bee can't fly." According to past theories of aerodynamics, the bumble bee's size, weight, and shape in relation to wing spread makes flying impossible. But, Mogensen goes on to emphasize, "The bumble bee, ignorant of this simple truth, flies anyway, and makes a little honey on the side."

Do-It-Yourself Thinking?

The *opportunity-maker* uses existing knowledge more productively. You may have heard of the individual who was given a rather complicated piece of new machinery to assemble. After a few hours, his supervisor returned with an instructional manual which she had forgotten to give the man. Much to the supervisor's surprise, the job was completed. She asked the worker how he could have assembled the machine without the manual. The man replied, "That wouldn't have done me any good, because I can't read. But I learned a long time ago that if you can't read, you have to learn to think."

George Bernard Shaw once claimed, "Few people think more than two or three times a year. I've made an international reputation for myself by thinking once or twice a week."

Our brain can perform like a machine if allowed. Fuel it up with facts, observations, problems, etc., and it can run day and night sparking out ideas (associations). These associations become the basis of our *ahas* in our problem solving.

Throughout this book we will deal with breaking old associations and forming new ones. It is the way cells grow in the body; it is the way ideas grow in the mind.

Do We Make Enough Associations?

Archimedes said that if given a lever long enough and a place to stand, he could move the world. *Associations* become the lever to move and solve the world's problems, as well as our own.

Duke Ellington, like many who behave creatively, was able to make connections rapidly and effectively. He was playing a concert at an outdoor festival when a low-flying plane noisily appeared above the grandstand. Duke changed the tempo to integrate the extraneous sounds of the engine and directed the plane along with the orchestra!

Children form new associations quickly and naturally, and they aren't afraid to express them. Their imaginations often formulate relationships that adults find amusing or annoying. A young girl surprised her teacher who was trying to clarify the meaning of the word "intervene." The pupil suddenly "lit up" and exclaimed, "I get it! It's like bologna in a sandwich!"

Let's extend the notion of mental associations a bit further. Take a moment and just *THINK*.

Think HARD!
Think FAST!
Think HARDER!
Think FASTER!

Are you aware of what was actually going on?

What Is Thinking?

Whatever it was you were *thinking* about, you were probably making associations by connecting one bit of data to another. The word *"think"* comes from the Latin *"cogitare"* (co-agitare, to turn in mind, consider, agitate). Hence when you *think hard and fast* you are probably shaking bits of data together mentally in your hope of making a relevant connection. For example, if you are trying to *think* of an acquaintance's name, you might shake loose a variety of thoughts related to the person — past occasions when you were together, associations you had made with him/her, etc. — hoping that something would suddenly connect with the correct name in your mental storage bin.

THE FAMILY CIRCUS

By Bil Keane

"You put the penny in and I'll flush it."

If you are *thinking* about a *new* use for a paper clip, you might associate it with a tie clip and thus generate the idea of using it as a tie clasp — maybe even gold-plating it for novelty jewelry. Or you might picture it opened to its full length and then associate it mentally with dry-cell batteries, as a connecting wire. You might even make the visual association to a racetrack, and then manipulate the material in your data bank until you come up with the *appropriate absurdity* of using it as a racetrack for fleas. Nothing earth-shaking, but rather a crude example of what is often called "creative" thinking. My friend once joked, "There is no such thing as creative thinking; there is only *thinking,* but it happens so seldom that when it does we call it creative!"

Perhaps the practice provided in this book will shake up the molecules in your brain, so that they may never fall back into exactly the same place, nor stay in one place very long as you *think* faster and faster about challenges and problems.

Let's consider the analogy of the kaleidoscope, wherein the more pieces of material we gather in the drum, the more possible patterns we can produce. Likewise, the more knowledge and experience that we allow into our brain, the more patterns, associations, or ideas we can generate.

However, merely gathering the knowledge — the bits and pieces in the kaleidoscope — does not guarantee the formation of new patterns. A winner on television's once popular *$64,000 Question* show understood this quite well. When this taxi driver was interviewed years later, he lamented his inability to use profitably the knowledge that he had stored, except on a quiz show.

As we must revolve the drum of the kaleidoscope to form new images, so must we manipulate the fragments of our stored knowledge to form new patterns — new *ideas.*

Is Our Brain More Than A Kaleidoscope?

Our creativity depends on our ability to interrelate not only what we already have accumulated, as with the kaleidoscope, but also the new data that we constantly draw in through our senses. The effectiveness of creative productivity also depends, of course, on the evaluation and development of embryonic ideas into usable, acceptable ideas.

Here's an example of how this kaleidoscopic notion works in a young child's mind. A kindergartener, who had not yet learned to read and write except for a few numbers and letters, frequently was embarrassed by forgetting events that were to take place in school.

One day she came home and announced to her parents, "We're going to a party, and I won't forget *when* because I wrote it down."

Her parents noticed the figure "22" written on the note she held. "You mean the 22nd? they asked.

"No," she exclaimed. "That's Tuesday! I wanted to remember Tuesday and I thought, Two's Day; 2s day! — so I put down a couple of 2s."

This is creativity at its simplest level — an example of combining what we know in new ways to solve a problem that may affect us individually. When an Einstein does it, he may get concepts which affect the entire world — like $E=MC^2$. Both examples show how concepts, whether simple or complex, are brought together in *relevant* ways. This may be quite contrary to what some people call creative where the associations are only original but hardly relevant.

Jot down a simple goal that you would like to reach today or this week. Set a deadline. Then see if you can come up with one new way of achieving it, by letting your brain associate around it as fast and freely as possible.

Can We Tap Our "Insanity?"

It is said that there is a fine line between genius and insanity. When the *insane* person can ground his/her mental associations in responsible reality, it often results in signs of genius.

An inmate of a mental asylum was sitting within the gates of the institution. On the outside, a man was changing the wheel of his car and stepped on the hubcap which contained the nuts he had removed from the wheel. The hubcap tipped over and the nuts dropped into a sewer on the side of the road. The driver swore and paced up and down in great distress.

Observing all of this, the inmate suddenly spoke up, "Why don't you take one nut off each of the other three wheels, and mount your wheel long enough to drive back to a service station where you can get the missing nuts replaced?"

The driver beamed with the sudden solution to his problem and exclaimed, "Say what is a man with a mind like yours doing in such an institution?"

The inmate quipped, "Mister, I'm in here for being insane, not stupid!"

Creative problem-solving becomes the task of finding the greatest number of interconnections and interrelationships among our vast and diverse internal and external resources, connecting them in both obvious and not so obvious ways. The more seemingly remote the relationship, the more the likelihood of originality in the idea. While it may take a great deal of creative thinking and effort to refine an original idea into a usable one, it often results in a breakthrough idea instead of a rather obvious adaption of what already exists.

CHAPTER FOUR

What Blocks Our Natural Creative Processes?

If our minds are so adept at sparking out new associations — at *kaleidoscopic speed* — what prevents us from generating new ideas every day? The blocks that get in the way are so numerous that it would be best to summarize them under two major categories: (1) anxiety about our ideas, and (2) conformity and habit-bound thinking.

Let us examine the chronological experiences that lead to anxiety about our ideas. The young child fearlessly blurts out whatever thought comes to mind, with no evident censorship. Fairly soon, however, the child learns "the facts" as adults see them. Whenever he/she thinks of a new idea or sees a new way of looking at something, the youngster is reminded of the "correct" view by the parent, teacher, or other authority figure. By the time the youngster reaches adulthood, he/she is usually well conditioned to look only to authorities for any thoughts or ideas of worth.

We tend to fear our own new ideas. Whenever we have conceived really new thoughts, others may have laughed, made us feel stupid or ridiculous, called us troublemakers, or told us not to rock the boat.

An official once reported that individuals who had made very few formal suggestions in his organization showed the fastest promotion rate, while those with a good suggestion record had a below-average promotion rate. It reminds me of a story I once heard about an executive telling his staff, "I want your frank and honest ideas; don't hold back, even if it costs you your job."

The next few cartoons illustrate very vividly how we learn to doubt the worth of our ideas at the earliest ages, and how our anxiety over our ideas is reinforced all through life.

"Now look what you've done!"

Drawing by Lorenz; ©1971 The New Yorker Magazine, Inc.

THE FAMILY CIRCUS   **By Bil Keane**

"Doggies can't be purple, can they, Mommy?"

© 1981 King Features Syndicate.
Reprinted with special permission of King Features Syndicate.

"Sure I want you to have opinions of your own. . . .
I just don't want to hear them.

Reprinted by permission of Bernard Lansky.

Copyright © 1996 Vision Enterprises, Inc.

© 1983 King Features Syndicate.
Reprinted with special permission of King Features Syndicate.

Think of some incidents in your own life that influenced your confidence in your own ideas. Begin as far back as you can remember and continue recalling such events at different ages or stages of your life. Ask yourself how those incidents may have affected your conformity patterns today. If you aren't able to recall any such incidents, you may be one of the fortunate few who escaped them.

Are You A Selective Conformist?

Basic to all attempts to nurture creative behavior is the attempt to break away from "blind" conformity, as differentiated from deliberate or purposeful conformity. For example, I purposely conform to driving on the right side of the road and hope that all others do likewise. However, I will not conform to some prevailing notions of educational practice or religious dogma. As one youth expressed it, "You can make me cut my hair, but you cannot make me cut my ideas!" In other words, conformity in behavior may sometimes be desirable or even necessary to a creative life, but conformity in *thinking* may not be.

I believe strongly in an adaptation of an old adage: "Give me the courage to change those things that should be changed, the strength to accept those things that should not be changed, and the wisdom to distinguish between the two."

When we conform to prevailing norms, we are seldom guilty of an error of *commission.* But what about errors of *omission?*

For example, on a sweltering July day, I was introduced to a formal luncheon group in a restaurant that was not air-conditioned. This was long before the time of the more current acceptance of informality in dress. Once I was introduced, I began my speech by taking off my suit coat and inviting all those in the audience to join me. My suggestion was greeted by a hearty round of applause. Yet had I not proposed it, I would have been perfectly safe, hardly likely to have been criticized. But the reaction I received proved that I would have committed an error of *omission* had I not extended the invitation once the thought occurred to me.

Errors of omission are much less likely to be detected than errors of commission. If I do not act upon an idea which later proves to have been *right,* I may be the only one aware of my mistake. However, if I act and am *wrong,* my error is usually obvious to others.

Most of us, through fear of ridicule or censure, tend to play it safe. Ideas are expressed only after we are sure of their worth and acceptance.

The extreme effects of culture on conformity is brought out in the classic psychological experiments wherein certain subjects went along with group impressions that were contrary to all logic and reason. For example, *planted* members of a group would each describe a shorter line as being longer than an obviously longer line. Some experimental subjects, after listening to the persuasive *plants,* agreed with the false judgment.

Blind conformity and unquestioning acceptance are traits which tend to stifle creativity. When we were children, "why" was one of the most common words in our vocabulary. But, the older we get, the more we tend to lose our inquisitiveness and accept everything at face value.

Conformity reduces the likelihood of creating fresh viewpoints necessary for creative insights. It is the enemy of originality and the creative productivity to which novelty can lead. To quote the late president John F. Kennedy:

Conformity is the jailer of freedom and the enemy of growth.

When Are You A Nonconformist?

The way in which we manifest conformity varies widely from one circumstance to another. For example, a scholar or researcher who behaves in a nonconforming way within his/her chosen discipline may behave more conformingly with respect to manner of dress or relationships with family members. An individual might respond very creatively to the challenge of constructing a centerpiece for a dinner party, while reacting very conventionally toward the selection and preparation of the food. An assembly line worker may behave ultraconventionally on the job, and yet produce exquisitely imaginative wood carvings in a home workshop.

With respect to conformity, it is well to consider the difference between (1) the nonconformist who honestly attempts to behave more effectively, and (2) the nonconformist who simply wishes to show people that he/she is different. The latter individual may be better described as a *counter-conformist* — or one who almost automatically does the opposite of what others do, right or wrong. There is also the pseudo-nonconformist who suddenly desires to be a nonconformist *like everyone else!*

How Habit-Bound Are You?

The pressures for conformity force most of us to form habit patterns that become unconscious parts of our thinking and behavior. In the behavioral realm we do things like shaking hands when meeting someone; this is a gesture which becomes a comfortable habit. We may not fully appreciate the comfort this action provides until we try to break the habit, as for example, when we are asked in a group session to greet people with our eyes rather than our hands.

Let's try a simple experiment. Clasp your hands in front of you and notice which thumb is on top. Now unclasp them and then reclasp your thumbs and fingers in the opposite manner, so that the other thumb is on top. How does this feel? Most people find it uncomfortable or unnatural to reclasp their hands in the new way, just as they would with the arm-folding experience described in Chapter 1.

Most of us find it strange, difficult or uncomfortable to change our customary way of doing things. And if trying to change a simple habit-pattern causes us discomfort, then imagine what happens when we try to change fixed ways of thinking or seeing things.

If I were to present you with a group of objects including a safety pin, bolts, washers, nuts, buttons, etc., and ask you to find a spring, you might hesitate or possibly give up. However, if I clipped the head and the point of the safety pin and left the now much more obvious "loop-spring" that remained in the assortment, you might see the spring immediately.

In a classic exercise, engineering students were given the task of getting a ping-pong ball out of a long, rusty pipe that had been welded upright to a laboratory floor. There was an assortment of hammers, pliers, rulers, soda straws, strings, bent pins, and an old bucket of dirty wash water in the room. After using the various tools and failing, most of the students discovered the solution of pouring the water into the pipe and floating the ball to the top.

The experiment was repeated with other students, with one important change. The bucket of dirty water was replaced with a crystal pitcher of clear ice water and glassware on a table with a decorative tablecloth. None of the students solved the problem because each one failed to associate the pitcher and ice water with the rusty pipe — a result of habitual ways of seeing things.

Challenge one of your longtime habits: try a new way of getting to work, or of expressing your affection for someone, or of celebrating

an anniversary, etc. Think about it for a few minutes and then plan your strategy.

One student challenged his routine way of traveling to school. He discovered that by using a variety of residential side-street routes, he could follow the refuse truck route early in the morning and pick up valuable castoffs at curbside. This turned his monotonous ride to school into an interesting and valuable event which he has continued to this day.

Never underestimate the strong pull that habit can exert. A New York City truck driver was on his way to a business address. When he arrived at the street he noticed that it was marked one-way, against him. So, he proceeded to the next block, went around and entered the one-way street from the proper end. As he approached the address he wanted, he suddenly realized that he was walking, rather than driving. Have you ever arrived somewhere, and then remembered that you meant to drive somewhere else?

On the other hand, not all habits are detrimental. Without habit, we would be like the proverbial centipede who got confused when asked to think about which foot came first when walking.

Are We Less Adaptive To Change?

John Gardner, in his book *The Temporary Society,* pointed out that each acquired attitude or habit, useful though it may be, makes us a little less receptive to alternative ways of thinking and acting. More and more we tend to do exactly what we've done best before, erring less often, but rarely finding new ideas for growth and development.

We tend to be *programmed* to see things in stereotyped or habitual ways and are frequently instructed in *the* way to do *everything.* An instruction booklet accompanying a toy doll is symptomatic of the problem: it began "How to Have Fun and Play with your New Doll." What unnecessary programming! It reflects the manufacturer's misunderstanding of children and their nonhabitual, nonstereotyped way of viewing things.

Well-Established Precedent: To sum up this discussion of conformity and habit-bound thinking, I have resurrected a classic poem written in 1895 by Sam Walter Foss. It tells it all in a way you won't forget.

One day through the primeval
wood
A calf walked home as good
calves should;
But made a trail all bent askew,
A crooked trail as all calves do.
Since then three hundred years
have fled,
And I infer the calf is dead.
But still he left behind his trail,
And thereby hangs my moral
tale.
The trail was taken up next day
By a lone dog that passed that
way;
And then a wise bellwether
sheep
Pursued the trail o'er hill and
glade
Through those old woods a path
was made.
And many men wound in and
out
And dodged and turned and
bent about
And uttered words of righteous
wrath
Because 'twas such a crooked
path;
But still they followed — do not
laugh —
The first migrations of that calf,
And through this winding
woodway stalked
Because he wobbled when he
walked.
This forest path became a lane

That bent and turned and turned
again;
This crooked lane became a road,
Where many a poor horse with
his load
Toiled on beneath the burning
sun,
And traveled some three miles in
one.
And thus a century and a half
They trod the footsteps of that
calf
The years passed on in swiftness
fleet,
The road became a village street;
And thus, before men were aware,
A city's crowded thoroughfare.
And soon the central street was
this
Of a renowned metropolis;
And men two centuries and a half
Trod in the footsteps of that calf.
Each day a hundred thousand
rout
Followed this zigzag calf about
And o'er his crooked journey
went
The traffic of a continent.
A hundred thousand men were
led
By one calf near three centuries
dead.
They followed still his crooked
way,
And lost one hundred years a
day;
For thus such reverence is lent
To well-established precedent.

CHAPTER FIVE

How Do We
Overcome The Blocks?

In order to experience what will be discussed in this chapter, allow yourself five minutes to list ideas for meeting a challenge that you have. Use a separate sheet of paper.

If we are to break habit-sets and move into new, original ways of viewing our problems and challenges, we must find ways to break old mental associations or connections and form new ones.

What Is Deferred Judgment?

Deferred judgment is a fundamental principle that can open us to the greatest flow of associations or connections of new ideas. It frees us from anxieties about the worth and acceptability or appropriateness of raw ideas as we conceive them.

This principle has been extensively researched. When used by groups in the idea-generating stage of the problem-solving process, it is commonly called brainstorming. The term was coined by its originator, Alex F. Osborn, and popularized in the 1950s.

The fundamental basis of deferred judgment, however, goes back as far as Ecclesiasticus in the Old Testament Apocrypha. One of its pithy sayings states: "Think first, criticize afterward." The great poet-philosopher Frederick Schiller expanded on this in 1788:

> Apparently, it is not good — and indeed it hinders the creative work of the mind — if the intellect examines too closely the ideas already pouring in, as it were, at the gates. Regarded in isolation, an idea may be quite insignificant, and venturesome in the extreme, but it may acquire importance from an idea which follows it; . . . In the case of a creative mind, it seems to me, the intellect has withdrawn its watchers from the gates, and the ideas rush in pell-mell, and only then does it review and inspect the multitude.[7]

The essence of deferred judgment is to allow a given period of time for listing all the ideas that come to mind regarding a problem, without judging them in any way. Forget about the quality of the ideas entirely and stretch for quantity. Combine or modify any of the ideas which have already been listed in order to produce additional ideas. Quantity and freedom of expression, without evaluation, are the key points which allow free reign to the imagination. Many of the psychological blocks caused by habit and past experience are broken down by the strange associations that take place during the "free wheeling" process of deferred judgment.

Deferred judgment involves looking at ideas and seeing where they might take us instead of merely trying to see what's right or wrong with them. The spontaneous associations which occur may help trigger important connections with knowledge and experience that we may have forgotten or repressed.

Deferring judgment also reduces the tendency to grasp frantically for the first idea or solution that reduces the anxiety of a situation. It leads to a wide search for alternatives — alternatives which ultimately provide a greater freedom of choice in making decisions. Furthermore, it can promote greater confidence in the decision, because there is less chance of having overlooked alternatives.

A classic example of the kinds of unique ideas that can emerge while deferring judgment involves packers of automobile parts who were wasting time reading the old newspapers used for packing material. The problem was to prevent this waste of time. Four ideas that emerged during a problem-solving session were: (1) hire illiterate packers, (2) use foreign language papers, (3) blindfold them, (4) hire blind packers. The fourth solution was adopted by the car manufacturer. Note the interesting associative process that seems to have led to the adopted solution.

What About Our Automatic Reactions?

It is often difficult not to have some kind of reaction to the spontaneous new ideas that enter our minds while deferring judgment. Whether this reaction is positive or negative, it need not prevent us from considering or simply listing the ideas. Although we may *react* to a new idea, we need not make any evaluation during the idea-finding stage. We might even jot down our momentary reaction as an additional idea. For example, if our unavoidable and immediate reaction to an idea is "too costly," we might note, "reduce cost," or "get some extra funds" as additional ideas.

Try your hand at deferring judgment for five minutes while listing as many ideas as you can regarding the challenge that you chose at the beginning of this chapter, or a new challenge if you prefer. Really let yourself go — experiment with the principle. Let your ideas flow as rapidly as they pop into your head. Later, you can look them over and see what you produced or where they led you. But for five minutes, just let them *flow,* as though automatically, from your head, through your fingers onto your sheet of paper. Draw a line to separate these ideas from your earlier ones.

Mentally "go with the flow," and see how many ideas you can generate. Make this a personal experiment. See if you can experience capturing anything that comes to mind, no matter how strange or even absurd. Have fun, Defer, Play, Flow! Alistar Cooke reminds us that:

Curiosity is free-wheeling intelligence.

How did you do? Did you experience a true release? Did you have some *ha has* as well as *ahas* as you went along?

How do your ideas compare with those during the first five minutes? In quantity? In quality? In potential value for development into useful ideas?

Research shows that significant gains are made using deferred judgment. However, if you didn't notice any apparent gain in the last experience, you might like to try again, perhaps with another person or persons. Explain the notion of deferred judgment first, and ask them to "let loose" with you. Part II will also provide additional opportunities for you to practice the principle again in a variety of useful ways.

Would You Like To Double Your Productivity?

Deferred judgment is deceptively simple to understand intellectually but extremely difficult to internalize. It takes practice, like any new skill.

Striking evidence of the value of practicing deferred judgment appeared in a study where we compared novices to experienced practitioners. Both groups were told to defer judgment, relate freely, strive for quantity of alternatives, etc. The experienced subjects, equivalent in all other respects to the naive group, outproduced the novices (in the same length of time) approximately two to one, on both quantity and quality of ideas as solutions to a problem. The results were highly significant statistically.

Artist Charles Burchfield exemplified the principle of deferred judgment in his style of painting. He kept a collection of over 1,000 ideas on scraps of paper. Furthermore, in completing a painting, he would paste over modifications of portions of the scene while attempting to achieve the effect he wanted. Once he casually remarked to an audience, "I don't know if these paintings are finished or not."

"Don't put off until tomorrow what you can do today," is an old adage that may be only partly true. The other side of the coin might be, "Don't make any decision today that can wait until tomorrow." Deferring judgment may lead to new ideas that can improve the decision.

The concept of deferred judgment is clearly differentiated from both *pre-judgment* and *no-judgment*. *Prejudgment,* or "prejudice," connotes premature closure that is unyielding to new input. *No-judgment* connotes total openness without closure or decision ever occurring. But, can we stay free of prejudice forever? Hardly, for we would never make a decision; we would continue to wait for still more facts to come in.

If we could speak of the *qualities* of "prejudiced, "nojudiced," and "deferjudiced," the term "deferjudiced" would imply taking an ever larger number of factors into consideration, in a given unit of time, before making a decision and taking action. The decision probably would be a better one, according to both research and the experience of those who practice this behavior.

"Deferjudiced" would also imply a willingness to reconsider the temporary "prejudices" that decisions represent when new data surface. Nothing is ever final — like the sign stating, "That's my decision and its *final* — for the moment."

Extended Effort?

Related closely to the deferment-of-judgment principle is a theory that extended effort in generating ideas tends to produce a greater proportion of good ideas among those generated later. Check your deferred-judgment list to see if you notice more intriguing, promising, or potentially valuable ideas showing up *later* on your list.

William J. J. Gordon, Chairman of Synectics Education Systems, describes "deferment" in the creative process as "the capacity to discard the glittering immediate in favor of a shadowy but possibly richer future." Like in long-term financial investing, we can forego the immediate reward of applying our first idea in expectation of an ultimately better solution.

How about investing another five minutes or so in the free flow of ideas regarding your challenge or a new one. Use the cartoon on the next page to help put you in a playful, free-wheeling frame of mind. Let it trigger associated thoughts for you.

Want A Few Idea-Stimulation Techniques?

The deferred-judgment principle might be thought of as the "environmental turnpike" that allows free flow to ideas that come to your mind. But what do you do when ideas *aren't* flowing? While the "turnpike" concept allows and encourages you to express ideas as they occur, you may often need to use other procedures which help to bring the ideas to mind in the first place, so that you do not become stranded on the turnpike, out of gas (like Snoopy at the typewriter). The following are some of the more productive techniques for triggering new ideas.

CHECKLISTS. In his classic text, *Applied Imagination,* Alex F. Osborn explains an effective checklist consisting of a series of verbs used to change mental attitude as one contemplates a problem or a challenge. For example, three of the verbs are: *magnify, minify,* and *rearrange.*

Suppose members of a family were trying to generate ideas on ways to enjoy their meals together more fully. If they were to think about the situation and apply *magnify,* they might come up with ideas like (1) inviting diverse people — foreign students, teachers, local artists, etc. — or (2) lengthening an occasional dinner by combining it with a favorite record album between courses. *Minify* might suggest (1) decreasing the size of the portions in each dinner course, but increasing the number of courses, so as to provide more variety and interest to the dinner or (2) eating around a very small table so as to make the whole dinner much more intimate or (3) eliminating the meal and feeding a needy family instead. *Rearrange* might suggest eating in the living room or on the porch, or having a reverse meal with the dessert first.

A recent idea in the pharmaceutical field is based on the *magnify* notion. It involves adding an emetic to the coating of drugs that pose a danger if used excessively — such as sleeping pills. Taken as prescribed, the small amount of emetic in each pill has no effect. If too many pills are ingested, the accumulated emetic from the coatings induces vomiting, thus "automatically" ejecting the overdose. In this example, magnification takes the form of adding or combining.

"Other men just sing in the bath."

In recent cost cutting efforts, a leading airline decided to remove the leaf of lettuce from under its vegetables in their meals *(minify)*. Employees noticed that passengers did not eat it anyway; savings — 1.5 million per year.

An Associated Press story dated June 1992, Indianapolis tells:

Former high school teacher Tom Killion has given a new twist to the lowly No. 2 pencil and turned it into the Bentcil®, a multimillion-dollar business *(rearrange)*.

Killion was teaching students about plastics in 1976 when the idea for a bendable pencil began to take shape.

"I worked with the concept of bending pencils because that would be drastically different," said Killion, who now heads Bentcil Co.

Working in his garage in his spare time, it took Killion two years to develop a pencil casing and writing lead that would bend without breaking. By heating compounds and bending them on a mold, the Bentcils could be shaped into flamingos, palm trees, sailboats — even the Golden Gate Bridge.

In his first year, Killion sold 500,000 Bentcils through mail-order catalogs. Business was so good Killion quit his teaching job in 1979 to devote 12-14 hours a day on his pencil.

Cartoonists frequently make use of the checklist verbs to create *appropriate absurdity,* the basis for their humor. For example, the cartoonist on page 49 used magnify and rearrange.

In all the examples and exercises throughout this chapter, remember that the first ideas conceived are only starting points. They can always trigger adaptations and related ideas that are more interesting and valuable than the original thoughts.

How about trying your hand at generating additional ideas for ways to enjoy (family) meals together more fully, or for one of your own challenges, based on the three idea-spurring categories. Remember, *defer judgment!* Anything goes!

Magnify: (Enlarge, multiply, add, increase, exaggerate, etc.)

Minify: (Subtract, divide, eliminate, shorten, simplify, etc.)

Rearrange: (Reverse, turn around, combine, substitute, scatter, etc.)

Now choose one idea that you like particularly and try to refine it into an idea that you can use.

FORCED RELATIONSHIPS. Another fundamental procedure involves taking anything in our awareness and attempting to relate it to the problem at hand. For example, in the previous meal situation, suppose the family focused on a tree outside the window. Someone might notice the leaves and suggest serving some element of the meal on attractive leaves; still another person might see highly-textured bark which might suggest small ice-carvings as table decorations.

Can We Use All Of Our Senses?

Forced relationships might involve senses other than sight. The family might focus on a bird twittering outside and attempt to force a relationship between that sound and the situation. It could prompt ideas such as introducing a music box for background sound-effects, or telling each other how they feel by humming accordingly.

Aside from using current sensations as stimuli for forcing relationships, we can use imaging to provide additional stimuli. We might imaginatively take a safari into Africa, and associate the meal with something there: plan a meal around the TV show, *Wild Kingdom;* "monkey around" with the way the food is served — the soup in glasses, the coffee in soup bowls, the ice cream on large platters, etc.; eat a picnic meal in a canoe or rowboat on a body of water. I have often stimulated groups that were running out of new ideas by encouraging them to take imaginary trips to one place or another.

Try to force a few relationships yourself now in regard to the meal challenge, or one of your own choosing. Again, *defer judgment!*

Anything may become relevant; creativity involves discovering the meaning in relationships that are not obviously relevant.

Deliberate or forced relationships may be *turned on* while conventional or habitual associations are shelved temporarily, or deferred. For example, if I ask you to associate a chair with a car, the obvious connection might be that both have seats.

If we examine the forced relationship further, we might observe that a car has wheels and ask, "Might a chair have wheels?" That may have sounded strange many years ago, but the idea is now commonly seen in the form of wheels or casters on chairs. If we stretched further, we might arrive at the even stranger association of the wheel on its side serving as the seat of the chair. From that somewhat bizarre notion might evolve the thought of the seat of the chair turning like a wheel. Suddenly we have conceived the idea of the now well-known swivel chair.

Can You Manipulate Your Images?

Thus, new relationships can frequently be forced by manipulating observations that we make, or images that we form in our minds. The inventor of the fork-lift truck reputedly conceived the initial idea while observing (and *magnifying*) the mechanism that lifts donuts into a donut oven.

Another inventor is said to have achieved his synchronization of the machinegun with the airplane propeller by visualizing how he threw rocks through windmill blades as a boy. His childhood experience suddenly became very relevant to his problem.

A final idea or product might not always evolve from one simple step, but from many channels of connections that open up after the initial forced relationship is made between seemingly unrelated items.

Think of the car or bus you ride. Focus on some part of it other than the seat or wheel. Now relate the part you selected to the chair you are sitting on. Defer judgment and play with it; visualize *magnifying* it, *minifying* it, *rearranging* it or a quality of it (the shininess of the bumper, for example) until you picture a connection that you might like to make with your own chair. If you don't come up with something you like, try it again later with different parts of the car or bus until something clicks for you. It is often especially exciting when your *aha* comes after stretching awhile.

ATTRIBUTE LISTING. Another commonly used process to aid the flow of ideas is called *attribute listing.* It involves taking specific aspects of an object or situation and then focusing particularly on the aspect selected. The checklisting or the forced-relationship processes can then be applied to whatever specific aspect is the subject of focus.

In the meal situation, we might look at the question of dessert, and examine everything we know about it — the shapes, colors, tastes, etc., of each specific dessert that we might think of. Then we might vary any one of those attributes or connect something else to that specific attribute.

Suppose we selected orange jello, cut into squares. One attribute might be that it was "soft and shimmery." If we focused on a brick in the fireplace and applied the hardness of the brick to the soft and shimmery quality of the jello, it might lead to the idea of freezing the jello and making it into a semi-icy dessert. The mental trip to Africa might suggest an animal-carving contest out of each one's jello before eating it. And so on.

Now try for a few ideas yourself on a different attribute of a particular dessert . . . or some other aspect of the meal . . . or some other challenge you might prefer. *Defer judgment,* and have fun!

Now choose one you like and try to refine it into an idea you can *use.*

MORPHOLOGICAL APPROACH. The morphological procedure applies the notion of *attribute listing* together with *forced relationship,* in a matrix approach. It speeds the production of countless ideas.

In the meal illustration, we might list some of the following attributes: people involved, places, times, foods, special effects, etc. Under each heading we would list a number of alternatives. For "people" we might jot down family, friends, strangers, needy people, celebrities, etc. . . . for "places" we might list different parts of the house, outdoors, picnics, campgrounds, etc. . . . for "times" we might list breakfast, lunch, dinner, snack-time, etc. . . . for "foods" we could list all kinds of different food items . . . for "special effects" we might have music, TV, odors, incense, etc.

Then we would take items at random from each of the headings (attributes) and connect them into a novel meal idea. For example, we might randomly select celebrity, basement, breakfast, hamburger, incense and put them together or adapt them in different ways: "incense" the "head of the house" by serving the kids hamburger for breakfast in the basement game room. Notice that we don't necessarily take the words literally. Incense suggested something different from a "special effect"; so did "monkey" in the earlier example.

Now form one or two random combinations of your own. Deferring judgment, see if you can interconnect other items from each list above into new meal ideas.

These processes can help us to break away from some of our habitual thinking — some of our rigidity— and to form new connections of thoughts. Remember though that these ideas are only starting points in the creative process. A great deal of refinement and development are usually necessary to make the ideas workable within the realities that exist.

The idea-stimulation techniques described here are examples of some of the main categories of methods used to help prompt the imagination. Many others will be used in the divergent stage of each step of the creative problem-solving process practiced later in the book.

At each divergent stage of the process, deferred judgment is used. Everything possible is done to maintain a constant flow of thoughts, whether these be the facts, problems, ideas, criteria for solution-finding, or the means of implementing and gaining acceptance. Research and practice have shown that the greater the flow of thoughts at each of these stages, the greater the likelihood of new insights and connections that become relevant as they are developed through the balance of the process.

What Is The Ultimate Purpose Of Deferring Judgment?

I must re-emphasize that divergent production — the creation of many unevaluated alternatives at each stage — is not an end in itself, but only a means to an end. Ultimately, judgment re-enters the scene, facilitating convergence, solution, and effective decision making — the ultimate purpose of the creative process.

What we are attempting to do is to get data out of memory storage and relate it to the current situation. So much of our problem-solving relies on data that is stored deep within us, data that we don't have in our present awareness and therefore fail to connect with the present situation. If we enable more of this data from memory storage to surface into our awareness, we are more likely to make rewarding connections. It is a "probability game" with no guarantees, but we are doing what Nobel Laureate Shockley calls "speeding up the hunch mechanism" by connecting things in many new ways.

CHAPTER SIX

Completing The Creative Process — From Ideas To Action!

Although we may see the infinite potential for spinning our mental kaleidoscopes, forming unlimited new associations or ideas, we are often unable to generate needed ideas on demand. We then turn to "incubation."

Incubation refers to that period in the creative process when we are not involved in conscious activity with respect to our problem. Often, during or after such a period, insights or ideas seemingly emerge from within us magically.

A pertinent example involved a little girl who had been trying unsuccessfully for several days to reinsert a rope-belt into her pajama bottom. One afternoon, while rushing in from play to get an ice cube from the freezer, the idea suddenly occurred to her that she could wet and "freeze" the rope into a circle or horseshoe. Then she could easily slide it through the opening in her pajamas.

Countless anecdotes in the literature recount instances of break-throughs in difficult problems when a person is detached from conscious attention to the problem. In fact, until the 1950s, the literature on creativity often suggested that incubation was the *only* way to generate creative solutions to problems. What we had to do was soak up data conscientiously and vigorously, and then simply wait for the ideas to miraculously occur between periods of deliberate effort.

But more recent findings in the study of creativity indicate that we *don't* always have to sit and wait for ideas to occur — as you may have seen for yourself in the previous chapter. Methods like those we have been practicing are designed to re-tap the flow of ideas when they seem to dry up. But, we can also turn to incubation.

By detaching ourselves during incubation we have deferred judgment or closure on the problem. As the problem "simmers" in the back of the mind or "on our back-burner," we attend to other things or problems and allow our senses full play upon our broader environment.

"If the answer should happen to come to me after school hours, I'll phone you."

Reprinted by permission: Tribune Media Services.

With respect to consideration of the problem, it might be reasonable to suppose that we are in a sort of hypnotic state; that is, we have given ourselves the suggestion to work on the problem and have then put it out of our consciousness. Input from our environment bombards the fringes of the problem until suddenly one element (such as the ice cube for the little girl) connects with an element of the problem and triggers it up into momentary awareness. This may occur in much the same way as a remote association is suddenly formed when we consciously attempt to produce ideas under deferred judgment. But note that the idea would not occur if the elements needed for the connection (beyond those observed during the incubative moment) were not implanted in the mind prior to incubation. Without the requisite links in our minds, we could be bombarded with apples while resting under a tree yet never come up with the law of gravity. We can dramatize this by pointing out that poems in Chinese do not occur to English poets.

Have We Overlooked Linkages?

Incubation enables the mind to attend to items of our past experience while we focus consciously upon other items in our present awareness. Links may be formed which are often overlooked when we search consciously for relationships. The conscious mind is limited in the number of ideas it can attend to at one time. Subconsciously, however, the mind is capable of much additional activity.

Let me demonstrate the way incubation works by using an analogy. Focus your eyes on an object. Now move your eyes a short distance and focus on another object near the first one. Can you still see the first object "in the corner of your eye?" This may illustrate how a problem remains "in the back of your mind," your subconscious mind. In this state, data that you might not combine intentionally becomes intermingled until an unusual combination or idea occurs. It may happen while you are involved in some other activity or even during sleep or rest.

When was the last time you tried the old trick of rubbing your stomach in a circular motion while patting your head simultaneously with the other hand? If you consciously start both operations at the same time, you may find it difficult or even impossible. However, if you begin one operation, continue it until it does not require conscious thought, and *then* start the other, you can usually handle the two operations easily. In effect, the first movement has been pushed into the subconscious, while the second operation is consciously being attended to. Incubation seems to work in a similar way.

The idea suddenly emerging from incubation will often be embryonic and fragmentary, sometimes quite strange. It seldom seems to be the complete answer to the problem.

For example, a physician was frustrated by the hazy information that patients gave about their condition when phoning during an emergency. One day, he suddenly visualized a heart patient calling him on the phone. When the patient tried to describe the strange rhythm of his heartbeat, the doctor commanded him to place the mouthpiece to his chest. The daydreaming doctor then imagined he heard the heartbeat. Snapping out of his reverie, he phoned a colleague and asked him to hold the mouthpiece to his chest. The doctor was disappointed not to hear a heartbeat.

The idea became a reality years later, however, after intensive study and development involving electronic engineers, among others. A special instrument was finally devised to enable a doctor to listen to the heartbeat over the phone. While a new idea may show promise, it may take time to evolve, so don't discard it.

Did You Write It Down?

A new idea may disappear just as quickly and mysteriously as it appeared. Did you ever think of an idea during a conversation and lose it before being able to communicate it? Or have you awakened with a solution, smiled with satisfaction, fallen back to sleep relieved, and later awoke but were unable to recall the solution? Because ideas frequently disappear, it is important to cultivate the habit of recording them immediately after they occur instead of trusting them to memory. Some people carry 3 x 5 cards or scraps of paper for that purpose. A dusty dashboard on a car can serve as a "dust-board" for recording unexpected ideas. A ballpoint pen can even record notes on the skin of your hand!

When Do We Stop Deferring And Begin Judging?

When viewing a problematic situation there is no end to the number of alternatives that could be generated by using the methods discussed in this book. Obviously, this alternative-searching could be carried to a ridiculous extreme, depending on the circumstances.

This chart portrays what probably occurs in creative action. In early and late intervals of time spent, relatively little productive gain is noted. The low end of the curve might be called "complacency" — willingness to accept common associations and habit-bound solutions.

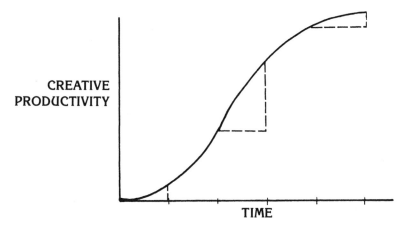

CREATIVE PRODUCTIVITY

TIME

Self-satisfaction often keeps us at the low end of the curve and prevents us from reaching out with our creative talents. If we tend to become smug about what we do, we lose sight of the improvements that could be made. I am intrigued by this anonymous quotation:

> If your own performance of a job looks perfect to you, it is not because you have done a perfect job, but simply because you have imperfect standards.

The upper end of the charted curve might be called "perfectionism," unwillingness to let go of an idea because it is not flawless. But perfection is only a nonattainable ideal; the best of anything is yet to be done.

So willingness to operate in the middle portion of the curve represents a happy compromise between staying "too tight" or being "too loose." It probably represents the area of maximum creative accomplishment. As Alex Osborn put it, "A fair idea put to use is better than a good idea kept forever on the polishing wheel!"

At some point toward the middle of the curve, we might well stop producing ideas and begin to evaluate them. During the evaluation (or solution-finding) phase we need to establish criteria — ways of judging — which serve as yardsticks to objectively measure the value of our ideas — how good or bad they are.

For example, if we are concerned with how long our ideas will take to implement, then we will select *time* as a criterion for evaluating each idea. If we are concerned with the amount of money required to implement, then *cost* becomes another criterion. Other possible criteria might be *effect on others* as well as *effect on ourselves.*

Just as we defer judgment in order to generate more and better ideas, it is likewise helpful to defer judgment as we think up more and better criteria beyond the obvious ones.

Try listing numerous criteria for evaluating those ideas that you generated earlier. Look at them from many different viewpoints; *defer judgment* while listing as many diverse criteria as you can bring into awareness.

Although your own criteria are likely to be more pertinent and specific, the following checklist of general criteria might help to trigger specific ones with respect to any particular problem that you happen to be pursuing: (1) effect on objective . . . (2) individuals and/or groups affected . . . (3) costs involved . . . (4) moral and/or legal implications . . . (5) tangibles involved (materials, equipment, space, etc.) . . . (6) intangibles involved (opinions, attitudes, feelings, aesthetic values, etc.) . . . (7) new problems caused . . . (8) difficulties of implementation and follow-up . . . (9) repercussions of failure . . . (10) timeliness . . . (11) fringe benefits . . . (12) ease of testing and taking first steps . . . (13) others you now think of . . .

By *deferring judgment* while we list many different criteria, we develop a better sensitivity to the possible effects of the ideas we are evaluating. If we consider all conceivable effects or repercussions of a new product or idea before we put it to use, we are less likely to find out later that there is something wrong with it. Even though you cannot go on listing criteria forever, any more than you can go on listing ideas forever, most people make the mistake of considering too few criteria rather than too many.

Can We Pretest Our Ideas Mentally?

The development of sufficient criteria enhances our sensitivity to new challenges or problems that might result from the implementation of new ideas. Criteria can help us recognize and appreciate shortcomings, deficiencies and loopholes. Sufficient criteria can help us prejudge whether ideas will work successfully in dealing with the problem.

By way of analogy, suppose we were building a worktable and we were seeking an appropriate piece of lumber for the top. If we had a large pile from which to choose, we would have certain considerations or "yardsticks" in mind as we looked through the selection — length, width, thickness, hardness, freedom from knots, freedom from warp, etc. Similarly, we must have certain considerations or criteria in mind if we are to do an effective job of selecting the most appropriate idea from among a whole "pile" of ideas on hand.

Since some criteria assume more importance than others, it may be advisable to group criteria in the order of their relative importance. Then we may even decide that while meeting some criteria is merely desirable, meeting other criteria is not only desirable but essential.

Oftentimes it would be appropriate to modify or refine our ideas before evaluating them against our criteria. The original ideas might be likened to raw materials, out of which we can form and polish solutions, and ultimately plans for action.

Originality in ideas is a necessary but insufficient condition for creativity. For example, if I were stretching for new uses for a coat hanger, an original or remote thought of using it as a ring for Saturn might surface. Refining this original thought might lead to the notion of making a ring-toss game.

It probably wouldn't serve much useful purpose to evaluate "ring for Saturn," an off-beat idea that emerged via deferred judgment, against criteria set for uses for a coat hanger. However, by adapting or refining the original idea, the ring-toss game might be judged seriously against the criteria.

Use the grid pictured on page 63, or your own adaptation. Under the IDEAS column, enter a few that you like best from the ideas you listed earlier. Under CRITERIA place several that you consider most important from those you listed. Rate all ideas under each criterion heading as either Excellent, Good, Fair, Poor, etc., until all blocks are filled. Choose the idea, combination, or adaptation that now looks most promising to you, and devise a plan for putting it into effect. Incidentally, you might adapt a poorly rated one by changing it to meet the criteria on which it failed. More on that in Part II and Part III, as well as other ways besides the grid for using criteria effectively for idea evaluation and development.

Deferred judgment often leads to strange but intriguing ideas which can then be put into realistic perspective. Some of these ideas can be adapted into workable and acceptable solutions which are better than anything else we have. And occasionally, the most prosaic idea still turns out best.

Reprinted by permission: Tribune Media Services.

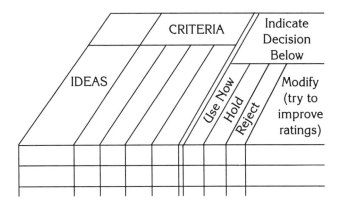

Summary

We have discussed sensing and defining problems, generating ideas, and then evaluating the ideas by applying criteria. Having carefully selected the most promising of our ideas, we might be tempted to feel that we have reached the pinnacle of success, that we have solved our problem. But rarely is this so; implementing a solution-idea almost always presents a new challenge of making our chosen idea acceptable.

The new "implementation-challenge" presents a continuing exercise in creative problem-solving, just as the case of our original problem for which we sought fresh ideas. It involves preparing our solution-idea for any problems that might arise during its application.

Drs. John A. Sellick Jr. and Joseph M. Mylotte, as well as other researchers at The Buffalo General Hospital, are involved in projects aimed at reducing nosocomial infections (infections acquired in a hospital) among patients and staff[8].

One study examined the number of needle stick injuries associated with recapping and discarding used needles. "We eliminated the need to recap needles by providing disposal containers in patient rooms, clinics, and other areas of the hospital," says Dr. Mylotte.

He notes that although the new protocol led to a significant decrease in the number of needle sticks, it was discovered that the containers created another problem.

To dispose of a needle, clinicians had to flip open a lid and drop in the instrument. According to Dr. Mylotte, as the container filled up, the needles did not lie flat but, in some cases, stuck straight up. "We found that some staff experienced needle sticks when they opened the lid to dispose of a needle," he explains. The problem was solved by changing to a different container that has a fixed opening on the top. "Now, staff simply drop needles into the containers, and the result is that we've been able to decrease such needle sticks by 75 percent," Dr. Mylotte remarks.

Although implementation frequently requires more creative effort than originating the idea, it *does* culminate in creative action and achievement, our ultimate goal. More opportunities to experience this will be provided in the next section as we apply the basic alternating process of *defer judgment, diverge, FLOW* and *stop temporarily, converge, DECIDE* within each phase of a five-step creative problem-solving process:

• Fact-Finding
• Problem-Finding
• Idea-Finding
• Solution-Finding (involving criteria-listing)
• Acceptance-Finding (or Implementation)

The problem-solving process outlined above may appear to be similar in terms of its steps or logical processes, to those formulated by philosopher John Dewey, psychologist Graham Wallace, and others. However, the plus ingredient introduced is the deliberate and exaggerated use of the imagination, a powerful force when effectively harnessed within a total problem-solving model.

The five steps are merely a guide rather than a strict formula for problem solving. Frequently a change of sequence may be introduced into the process; and it is always advisable to provide plenty of opportunity for incubation. The main emphasis throughout each step is to *accumulate alternatives* before zeroing in on the better ones. And remember that nothing is final, for every solution presents many new challenges.

Intellectualizing the creative problem-solving processes is different from internalizing them effectively — just as attending a lecture on physical education is different from attending a program *for* physical education.

How's Your Attitude?

On the final day of one of our Creative Problem-Solving Institutes, a company executive remarked, "If you could only have gotten us into this frame of mind on the first day, we could have accomplished so much more!" I explained that a major objective of the Institute was to develop just such attitudes as he was now experiencing. I also explained that we had *talked* about attitudes in our orientation session, but then proceeded to provide *experiences* that developed the desired frame of mind in the participants. Simply talking about it at the beginning of the Institute hadn't produced the desired change.

"Aha," exclaimed the executive, "I see now, that you have certainly accomplished your objective." He realized that he was then ready to take advantage of the new viewpoints and attitudes in facing his company's problems.

How Important Is Practice?

You may have to practice using the creative problem-solving procedures for some time before you become comfortable and productive with them. I question whether a person can fully understand or fully appreciate the meaning of concepts like deferred judgment until he/she has experientially internalized them. Part II will help you do just that.

PEANUTS reprinted by permission of
United Feature Syndicate, Inc.

CHAPTER SEVEN

Introduction To Part II:
Warming Up To The Full Process

This part guides you through a number of creative problem-solving experiences involving challenges or problems that *you* set for yourself in each chapter. In each case, stretch for maximum *sensitivity* to the desires, challenges, opportunities, or problems in your life. You may discover many opportunities to explore that you hadn't thought of before.

Each succeeding chapter provides you with fewer and fewer cues to trigger your imagination and to guide you through the alternating process of "flowing" and then "deciding" at each of the steps. If you find that the cues are more than you need for the desired flow and resulting *ahas,* then progress at your own pace or move ahead to the next chapter, where less cues are given.

Unless you are truly distracted from your flow by the cueing, I urge you to go through all of the chapters so that you may pick up some fine points as well as experience more and more stretching. This groundwork should help you to feel more comfortable and effective when you "go it alone" in Chapters 11 and 12.

Are You Willing To Stretch Your Mental Muscles?

Each step of the process gives you another opportunity to achieve some new and relevant associations — *ahas* — the heart of the creative process. If you skip a step, you can still reach a solution, but it is less *likely* to be a good, workable one. Likewise if you don't *stretch* for many alternatives in each step, you can still find your solution — but it may not be as effective as if you thought up a greater amount of alternatives from which to choose. There is no *guarantee* that following a step, or stretching within it, will produce an important *aha;* however, extensive research and practice has consistently demonstrated the *probability* that you will find more and better *ahas,* resulting in better solutions or decisions. You will be less apt to be confronted with superficial solutions or those that deal with symptoms rather than underlying causes.

Perhaps you can experience what I'm talking about rather quickly and simply by trying the following introductory experiments:

- List a challenge or problem you have . . . not one that is "earthshaking," but simply one where it would be "neat" if you could find a new way of dealing with it . . .

- Now jot down your first reaction as to what you should do about it . . .

Did you have an *aha?* If you did, be grateful! It's like hitting the jackpot with one try. But chances are that you didn't, since *ahas* rarely are that simple.

- Now, jot down something you know — are aware of — about the challenge or problem . . .

- Next, define the problem as you see it . . .

- Now, state your way of solving it . . .

- Next, state your reason for deciding on that way . . .

- Finally, note how you will put your solution into effect . . .

Any *ahas* that time? It could have happened as you, in a sense, went through the five steps very quickly, reacting to your first thought in each step. But it's not very likely.

Now try breaking past the immediate connection you made at each step by adding three or four more thoughts — different alternatives — under each step; *defer judgment* as you allow several alternatives to flow freely in each step.

- Fact-Finding (what you know about it):

- Problem-Finding (different ways of viewing or defining the problem): Try to start each definition with the words, "In what ways might I . . .":

- Idea-Finding (ideas that might help solve it):

- Solution-Finding (criteria for evaluating the ideas — means for judging — reasons the ideas are good or bad):

- Acceptance-Finding (ways to get my best idea(s) into effect):

- Plan of Action (choose the best way(s) to get your selected idea(s) into effect; add a timetable for carrying out your plan):

Let's hope that you caught a worthwhile idea that time, and came up with a new and relevant plan of action. If you didn't, some of the experiences that follow will help to increase the probability that it will happen the next time.

Before we begin our full stretch in the next chapter, try one more quick creative problem-solving run-through. This time we will emphasize "right-brain" focus — imagery — almost totally. In all subsequent chapters, we will combine the verbal and the imagery constantly as we stretch and flow through the process.

Have You Tried Relaxation?

Choose another "non-earthshaking" challenge or concern. Then take a moment to relax yourself fully from head to foot. Try to *tighten* each muscle as totally as possible, then let go so that you can experience release of the tension in each individual muscle. Check once more for any remaining tension. If you find any, concentrate on that spot by tensing the muscle even more and then letting go.

Now, in a more relaxed state, proceed to image as follows, making notations or sketches when significant thoughts occur.

- **Fact-Finding:** Visualize the situation or challenge you have chosen. "See" in your imagination everything you know about it. Watch what is happening, who or what is involved, when, where, how, and why it is happening. Let the pictures flow through your mind as in a dream.

- **Problem-Finding:** Now fantasize or "daydream" a scenario as to how you would *like* the situation to look. What would your *wish* be about the situation if you could wave a magic wand and alter it any way you'd like? Imagine it *that* way.

- **Idea-Finding:** Begin changing some of the details in the picture of the situation as it *presently exists* to make it more like what your fantasy-wish portrayed. Change the original picture bit-by-bit. Magnify, minify, or rearrange parts, or all of it, in ways that bring it more and more toward your ideal fantasy. (You might like to do this by visualizing your fantasized scenario on one TV screen and the situation as it presently exists on a second screen. Then start modifying the present picture as explained.) Don't be intimidated by any past conditioning that you may have experienced about fantasizing, daydreaming, wishing, etc.

Now focus on the changes you seem to like most.

- **Solution-Finding:** *Picture* and *feel* how you might react to the kinds of changes you selected, as well as how others might feel or react. "Jump into their skins" and picture your selected changes from *their* points of view, from as many viewpoints as possible.

- **Acceptance-Finding:** Keeping those multiple feelings and reactions in mind, begin picturing some of the modifications that might make your fantasy more workable or acceptable to yourself and others. Piece together the best image of yourself dealing effectively with the original challenge or concern. Try for as much detail as you can.

Then make notes of the best action plan that you have now created, including a timetable for carrying out the plan.

With a bit of stretch, you *may* have had an *aha,* even if only a five- or ten-volt one, that may have led to a worthwhile plan for dealing

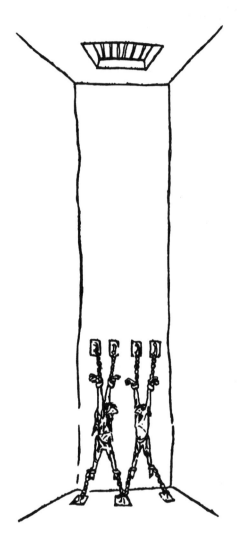

"Now here's my plan . . ."

with at least a small part of the challenge. If you didn't, the extensive stretch called for in the next chapter is almost bound to generate a few *ahas* on your next problem-choice.

Can We Habitually Break Habits?

Psychologists sometimes raise the question of whether learning specific methods of solving problems may create "sets" or fixed habits that interfere with a way of solving a particular problem. It is precisely *against* any such rigidity — such interference with flexible associations — that this book is designed. In a sense, it attempts to establish habits *against* habits (a set *against* set) when approaching new situations, yet ones which allow a person to live, in full awareness, with certain temporary sets or habits required in our society.

Instead of merely reacting in a habitual way to your awareness as you may have done on top of page 67 earlier, you can learn to:

- re-examine the situation for more facts;

- re-define the problem (it probably isn't the same as you first thought);

- generate alternative ideas as reactions or responses to the problem as now viewed;

- become aware of the multiple repercussions or consequences associated with the ideas being considered; and

- develop the best idea as fully as possible before putting it to use.

In the next chapter you may be doing this in an exaggerated way, but by Chapter 11 it should become natural to you. Hopefully, you will make it a *habit* to automatically *break* habit in forming mental associations, so that you may see new and relevant opportunities, solutions and decisions.

CHAPTER EIGHT

How About A S-T-R-E-T-C-H Through The Process?

This chapter will provide you with an opportunity to stretch your creative processes in many diverse ways in sensing and solving your problems. You will expand greatly on what you did in the previous chapter as you take charge. I will merely offer stimuli that may increase the *probability* of your deriving some *ahas*. These *ahas* should serve to reinforce you in modifying your thinking-behavior to include more and more of the emphases suggested.

The deliberate development of creative behavior might be viewed as an *exaggerated* push for change. We assume that the imagination regresses, when it is not prodded, to more natural and desirable levels that contain a reasonable balance between imagination and judgment. Stretching beyond the normal limits of our imagination serves to make it possible to ease back to a more natural level, as a bent tree finally does when we release it from an "overstretch" in the other direction.

The experience that follows will serve as an example of one of the infinite number of "compositions" that might be conceived by putting the pieces of the process together in a variety of arrangements, just as an infinite number of musical compositions can be generated by rearranging the notes within various theoretical frameworks.

As I provide the stimuli for your thoughts, allow them to *flow* freely without analyzing or evaluating them in any way. Don't let anything inhibit your thoughts.

Allow yourself at least an hour-and-a-half to two hours on this chapter. If you are pressed for time, plan an incubation break and finish it at a later time. You will be working on something important to you so you should allow yourself all the time you need.

If you should happen to solve a problem to your satisfaction early in the process, proceed to another challenge. Should you find that you are accomplishing something important and my stimuli are interfering with it, leave the book and work ahead however you like while you are flowing productively. Check back later to see what special techniques I added, and use them on another challenge if you wish.

What Is Our Objective?

Remember that the objective is to *accomplish* something valuable to *you*. My diverse stimuli are designed to increase that likelihood. Do not read ahead before responding to each instruction, unless you are only interested in understanding what I am doing rather than experiencing your creative processes. If you should decide to read only and not to record as suggested, I urge you to at least *think* your responses to each instruction before reading on.

Please don't try to figure out the rationale for the particular stimuli I chose; each is merely a way of potentially tapping new flow, new associations. Just *respond* spontaneously, and then go back later and analyze if you wish.

Be aware that this exercise is often given at the completion of a creative-studies course or Creative Problem-Solving Institute after intensive practice in processes designed to increase the flow of ideas. So, speed is not important right now. Just move along from item to item, trying always to *allow* your thoughts to flow wherever they take you in response to my stimuli. And if something is not clear to you, make whatever sense of it you can at that moment and respond to that without further worry. Good luck in your adventure!

Now, let's sensitize ourselves to challenges in our lives.

DISCOVERING CHALLENGES:

1. List, sketch, or symbolize any desires or challenges you have in any aspect of your life.

2. After you "run dry," extend yourself by jotting down additional thoughts as they are triggered by the following questions:

   What would you like to do, have, accomplish?
   What idea would you like to get working?
   What do you wish would happen?
   What relationship would you like to improve?
   What would you like to do better?

What do you wish you had more time for?
What do you wish you had more money for?
What more would you like to get out of life?
What are your unfulfilled goals?
What turns you on?
What angered you recently?
What makes you tense, anxious?
What misunderstandings did you have?
What have you complained about?
With whom would you like to get along better?
What changes for the worse do you sense in attitudes of others?
What would you like to get others to do?
What changes will you have to introduce?
What takes too long?
What is wasted?
What is too complicated?
What "bottlenecks" exist?
In what ways are you inefficient?
What wears you out?
What turns you off?
What would you like to organize better?

3. List at least six roles that you play in your life (example: daughter, politician, student, etc.).

4. Now *imagine* yourself in each role and make notes of any more desires or challenges that come to mind.

5. Imagine sending a *nonverbal* message to a co-worker regarding his/her behavior. Imagine how you might feel doing it. Then add more challenges to your list.

6. Choose one challenge, desire, concern, or idea that you would most like to start doing something about.

FACT-FINDING:

1. List, sketch, or symbolize what you know about the desire, concern, challenge, or idea chosen.

2. Let the following questions trigger more data about the situation:

   What *is* or *is not* happening?

   Who *is* or *is not* concerned?

   When *does* or *doesn't* this occur?

   Where *does* or *doesn't* this occur?

   Why *does* or *doesn't* it happen?

   How *does* or *doesn't* it happen?

3. Make sure you've noted how you and others do and do not *feel* about the situation. This is an important part of the data. Try to *understand*, not necessarily agree. Imaging yourself inside the other person's skin, experience vicariously the feelings of that other person. *Defer judgment* as you record all the feelings you become aware of.

4. Glean more data from your memory. Your senses can help trigger this. For example, the sense of smell is one of the most powerful triggers for awakening memories. Try smelling deeply a variety of odors emitted from foliage, spices, perfumes, ashes, or other items from the immediate environment. Deal with each slowly, reflecting, ruminating as you breathe in each aroma. Record any thoughts or memories that the fragrances "trigger." Try the same with listening to music, tasting, etc.

5. Connect to your earlier facts whatever you can from the thoughts you just recorded.

6. Let's get to more data about *ourselves*. Make notes of your *strengths,* modesty aside. Brag about your personality, your abilities, etc. Think of any compliment or appraisal anyone ever gave you. Look for elements of strength that they stated or implied.

7. Now add new thoughts that may surface as you contemplate those strengths. These thoughts and feelings can be considered part of your data.

8. Don't hesitate to add as many thoughts as occur to you as you think of any further strengths and their implications.

9. Experience your immediate environment through *all* of your senses, just as you did earlier in smelling, etc.: look, listen, taste, touch, smell. Then add any thoughts that surface from your memory bank — facts that may be relevant but were forgotten.

   NOTE: Our mind has a remarkable capacity to *store* data as compared with its relative inability under normal conditions to *retrieve* that information. We have much more information than we realize, if only we can "shake it loose."

10. Try *imaging* the desire, challenge, concern, or idea that you have been describing. Close your eyes and imagine it as fully as you can. "See" it, "feel" it, "hear" it, "taste" it, "smell" it. Use your imagination to note details as fully and as vividly as you can.

PROBLEM-FINDING:

1. Flow with as many questions as possible surrounding the situation that you described. Try to start the questions with the words, "In what ways might I . . . ?" "What might I do to . . . ?" "How might I . . . ?" If "Should I" questions come to mind, change them to "In what ways might I decide . . . ?" If questions calling for more facts occur, word them as "In what ways might I find out . . . ?" Let your thoughts flow without analyzing or judging the appropriateness of each problem-statement you list.

THE FAMILY CIRCUS

By Bil Keane

"I was just dreaming — y'know, when you close your eyes and the picture comes on?"

2. Now think of a "peak" joyous experience in your life. Close your eyes and relive that experience in your imagination. Daydream it.

3. Relate this vicarious experience, or aspects of it, to your current situation. What made it peak? How might that suggest new, current challenges? List additional "In what ways might I . . . ?" statements of your problem as a result of connections you might make with the peak experience you imaged.

4. Stop a moment and ask, "What is the *real* problem? The *essence* of it? "What is my basic objective?" "What do I want to accomplish here?" Ask "Why" of each question you have listed: "Why do I want to do this?" Then answer, "In order to . . . " As a result of these questions and answers, try to restate and broaden your problem. For example, if you asked "Why" of the problem, "How might I catch the mouse?", it might lead to the answer, "In order to get rid of it." This leads to the restatement, "How might I *get rid* of the mouse?" The latter allows for more possibilities. List several restatements of your problem.

5. Draw a personal symbol to represent yourself.

6. Now write additional "In what ways might I . . . ?" questions connecting interpretations or feelings about the symbol to the situation you are defining.

7. You start out in any perplexing situation with a "mess." You find the "fuzzy" challenge within the "mess" and then you state the challenge as broadly as possible, as in 4 above. The broad problem then breaks down into a number of subproblems. Break down your earlier questions into aspects, parts, stages, operations, etc. List more "In what ways might I . . . ?" questions that get at specific aspects of the problem — such as "In what ways might I use available resources more fully?"

8. Try once more to imagine the details of the challenge, problem, or idea you are working on. Close your eyes and see how many facts or data you can picture in your imagination.

9. What do you wish would happen concerning the observations that you made when using your imagination? List as many wishes as you like, with no restraints or judgment.

10. Convert each wish into additional "In what ways might I . . . ?" problem-statements. For example, if you wished that the budget hadn't been cut, you might list, "In what ways might I accomplish objectives with limited funding?" "In what ways might I recoup funds by cutting waste?", etc. If you wished that you were younger, you might record, "In what ways might I look younger?", etc. Try seeing it in several new ways.

11. From among *all* of those that you have listed, select the "In what ways might I . . . ?" question which looks most promising or interesting to work on *first*. Try to make the best choice for *now* — a starting point for your idea-finding efforts at this moment in time. Save the other problem-statements that look promising or important to you for another time.

    NOTE: Even now the other statements are likely to work subconsciously to trigger related ideas, since you have "loaded your computer" with these diverse ways of viewing the problem.

IDEA-FINDING:

1. *Deferring judgment* as fully as you can and allowing your ideas to flow freely, list, sketch, or symbolize as many ideas as possible for attacking the problem you just chose.

2. Magnify, minify, rearrange, etc., in seeking additional ideas. Ask yourself what would happen if you made something bigger, smaller, reversed elements or positions, etc. Visualize each of these

The Saturday Evening Post
© 1965 The Curtis Publishing Company

"I just hope it isn't a contact lens."

The Saturday Evening Post © 1965.

changes. As you imagine them, do not evaluate the ideas that occur; just continue to jot them down.

3. In searching for additional ideas, look for strange analogies to the situation that you are working on. For example, if the situation has to do with the office or home, think of a "circus" or a "spaceship" and draw relationships from these other settings. If it involves a person, use animals, plants, or machinery for analogies; if it involves technology, use people or other living things; etc.

4. Listen to music with a "descriptive" quality that will tend to stir some response from you. Hum or sing it if none is available to you now. Concentrate on the music and forget about what you have been writing; "incubate" momentarily on the problem. Try moving physically with the music in some new way. Make new "physical connections," if only with your head, fingers, toes, etc.

5. As the music concludes, write or sketch more ideas that come to mind. See if your body movement suggested anything, even symbolically.

6. Close your eyes, and imagine yourself in your own "personal paradise." Then write or sketch more ideas, connecting aspects of your personal paradise with the problem that you are working on.

7. Take other imaginary trips (or actual ones, if time is unlimited) through your favorite department store, museum, zoo, etc., and connect aspects with the problem at hand.

8. Try to "force" relationships with what you see, feel, hear, smell, taste in your present environment, triggering and noting additional ideas.

9. Looking back at some of the ideas that seem interesting, *imagine* each one as though it existed, as though it were actually taking place. Try to magnify, minify, and rearrange each idea in your imagination in as many ways as possible, deferring judgment and jotting down modifications or new ideas that emerge.

   NOTE: You are still attempting to add to your *total* idea-finding list, out of which you will then select ones to evaluate and develop. So, don't hesitate to continue jotting down strange or wild ideas.

10. Choose from your total list the idea(s) or combinations that look most promising or interesting and/or that you *like* best at this time. The choice may be totally "gut-level," even if you have no awareness of how your selection can be implemented.

    NOTE: If your original problem-statement was quite broad, you may find that many of your ideas are really "subproblems." For example, consider the problem "In what ways might I become more effective in my job?" You might respond with, "learn more about the entire organization and how it interrelates," "develop my professional skills," etc. These, in turn, would become "specific approaches" — subproblems — for further probing ("In what ways might I learn more about the entire organization and how it interrelates?" "In what ways might I develop my professional skills?") before continuing on to solution-finding.

SOLUTION-FINDING:

1. List, sketch or symbolize evaluative criteria to assist you in judging how "good" or "bad" the ideas you just chose are for meeting the challenge you have been working on in this chapter. Consider who or what might be affected, elements that might make it fail, or those that might make it better.

2. In your imagination, be something in the situation other than yourself. Become another person, an animal, or a thing, imagining how the ideas look from that point of view. Then add additional criteria from the new connections that you make.

3. List as many "Will it . . . ?" questions as you can. "Will it cost too much?" "Will it adversely affect someone?" etc.

4. Visualize others reacting as you tell them about your ideas. See their expressions, their "nonverbals." Then add any further criteria that you become aware of.

5. Review all the criteria that you have recorded. Choose those you feel are most important, adding any you wish from the checklist of general criteria on page 60.

6. Set up a grid to evaluate all the ideas that you are considering against each criterion that you selected. Get a more objective picture of each idea's potential. Use any rating system you like: letters, numbers, or even smiles or frowns in each rating box.
   NOTE: If you should discover now or during Acceptance-Finding that your favorite idea has some shortcomings that you hadn't been aware of, that can be an important *aha* too. We might call that a *negative aha.*

ACCEPTANCE-FINDING:

1. Work now with the idea you would most like to use first for meeting the challenge you have been working on in this chapter. If it doesn't generally meet the criteria, "tailor" it to fit them. Fantasize it working, then adapt the fantasy to reality by modifying it as necessary. Use the criteria as "tools" to work your raw ideas into usable ones. For example, if "money" is an important criterion on which the idea rates poorly, record ideas under such new questions as "In what ways might I reduce the cost of this?" "In what ways might I find more money for this?" *Defer judgment,* recording all ideas that occur.

2. *Defer judgment* and produce a free flow of suggestions for gaining acceptance and putting your idea to use — suggestions that aid in implementing, insuring success, improving the original idea, showing its advantages, gaining enthusiasm of yourself or others,

"What's the opposite of 'Eureka!'?"

Drawing by Dana Fradon; © 1975 The New Yorker Magazine, Inc.

overcoming objections, anticipating possible misconceptions, pretesting, etc.

3. Close your eyes. Concentrate on physically relaxing yourself from the top of your head to the tips of your toes, thus providing another moment of "incubation." As you discover points of tension, try tensing the muscle *even more;* then relax it fully.

4. Close your eyes again. Visualize modifications as you adapt your idea to suit all those concerned. In your mind, notice your reactions and expressions, as well as those of others. Keep on adapting the idea until everyone seems to feel good about it — until both you and the others smile happily. Record the adaptations you made.

5. List additional ways of getting your idea to work. Emphasize *specifics,* particularly those which are *verifiable* or *demonstrable.* For example, change "cut down on smoking," to "smoke one cigarette less each succeeding day until I've stopped entirely." Apply the checklist, "Who, what, when, where, why, how": Who might help? What other people and groups? What resources might I use? What special times, occasions, or places? Why might they want to do it? How might I get their cooperation?, etc. *Defer judgment* as you flow freely with your ideas.

6. Think of your favorite food, sport, or hobby. Try to relate something from any one of these to the idea you want to get working effectively. *Defer judgment* as you jot down associations.

7. Choose ideas you can use from the entire Acceptance-Finding list even if they deal with only one small part of the problem or challenge.

8. Now spell out *in detail* a plan *for the moment.* List as many *specifics* as possible, including first steps you will take, schedule

of follow-ups, etc. What will be your one orange? Be sure to include something that you will *do* physically before tomorrow night that will commit you to action. It might be an initial phone call, contact, letter, purchase, movement, etc. Also schedule among your next steps a time when you will come back to other problem-statements or ideas you recorded in this chapter. And, of course, continue to incubate for additional ideas that may be implementable as you move forward with your plan.

9. Close your eyes. Relax as fully as you can. Imagine yourself lying comfortably in a lounge chair, a hammock, a haystack, a rowboat, or the like. Before you is a large TV set which you can manipulate from a remote control in your hand. Turn on the TV and see yourself putting your plan into action just as you would like to see it happen. See every detail, every expression and reaction, yours as well as those of others involved.

10. Now bring into the "picture" an unexpected development. For example, a key person moves from your city. Using your imagination, "watch" the consequences. How is contact maintained? Who helps fill the role?, etc.

11. Add further adaptations to your recorded plan, taking into account what you just "saw" so as to further insure the effectiveness of your plan.

12. Image and record new challenges that might result from implementing the plan.

13. As a final step, make any modifications desirable as a result of the new challenges you just listed. We nearly always find that before solution-ideas can be utilized or implemented, they need to undergo some changes in order to fit our needs precisely; that is, in order to cope with challenges that might arise in applying the ideas.

    NOTE: This process resembles the one used in the clothing business. A garment progresses from the drawing board and fabric to the model, then to the purchaser, after which it must be tailored to the customer's dimensions. Likewise, we tailor an idea carefully before applying it. Early tailoring of an idea may be relatively easy and inexpensive compared with later action often required to rectify a defect in an idea.

Is Your Plan Ready To Stand On Its Own?

We are like parents to our creative ideas. As with children, we want to prepare them to "weather" the needs of the practical life. Implementation involves preparing our ideas for any demands that may be made on them or from any problems that might arise in their use.

A solution or a plan of action might be likened to a landing on a stairway, a place to rest; a place to get a perspective of our position and our direction, to see where we are going and where we have come from in our thinking.

Unfortunately many people fail to view their solutions this way. A dramatic example of the opposite way of viewing them is the statement, in an advertisement, by R. E. Olds, Designer of the "Reo the Fifth" automobile in 1912:

Reo the Fifth — the car I now bring out — is regarded by me as pretty close to finality. Embodied here are the final results of my 25 years of experience. I do not believe that a car materially better will ever be built. In any event, this car marks my limit. So I've called it My Farewell Car.

And of course, Reo's are no longer on the market!

An example illustrative of how new challenges emerge from present "solutions" involves a team of electronics engineers who had the problem of designing a special-purpose camera. They created a camera that met the special needs very effectively. Since the camera was very costly and could not be used as generally as might be desired, the emerging challenge was to reduce the cost. By creatively approaching this challenge, they were able to reduce the cost drastically. This in turn created new challenges in selling the camera to broader markets. And so on. One "solution" becomes another challenge. Thus every creative solution paves the way for more opportunities for the alert and aware problem solver.

How About Incubation?

I hope you gained some new insights into the concern you chose to deal with. If you didn't, then let incubation play a stronger role. Get away from it for a while and let new associations be triggered by random input from other daily activities. Keep pad and pencil handy in order to catch those fleeting thoughts that may well up into your consciousness.

Later today or tomorrow, look over what you wrote in this chapter, including the challenges associated with implementing the idea you would like to use. Also review carefully problem-statements or ideas other than the first ones you chose, to see whether new possibilities emerge. Play imaginatively with what you wrote or what you captured during incubation. See whether new directions become apparent toward a viable solution and a plan of action.

If nothing emerges, try another period of incubation. Continue alternating between deliberate involvement with the challenge and a period of conscious detachment that allows the incubation process to take over. This alternating procedure should increase the likelihood of a breakthrough or a new insight, as compared with working doggedly on the problem or relying only on the chance association during incubation.

Remember, it is a probability game that we are playing. We may not be able to *guarantee* ourselves an insight or solution, but we can significantly increase the *probability* of finding it. Repeated research and experience has borne this out.

THE NOW SOCIETY

Are you in the creative process or could
you take out the garbage?

CHAPTER NINE

Are You Ready For Accomplishing With Less Prompters?

Wait until you are fresh and rested before beginning this second run-through of the process. Your timing can have significant bearing on your results as well as on your enjoyment of the process.

This time choose another challenge, desire, concern, or idea that you would like to *do* something about. It could be something from the list you created on pages 73-74 earlier, or something that emerged from that entire experience.

FACT-FINDING:

1. List, sketch or symbolize *facts* and *feelings* about the situation you have chosen. See how much you can record about it in a free-flowing, deferred-judgment manner.

   What *is* or *is not* happening?
   Who *is* or *is not* concerned?
   When *does* or *doesn't* this occur?
   Where *does* or *doesn't* this occur?
   Why *does* or *doesn't* it happen?
   How *does* or *doesn't* it happen?

   Flow with these facts and feelings.

2. Try visualizing the challenge, desire, concern, or idea you have been describing. Close your eyes and imagine it as fully as you can. "See" it, "feel" it, "hear" it, "taste" it, "smell" it. Try for as clear a mental picture as you can image. Add as many more details as you are now able.

PROBLEM-FINDING:

1. Try for as many as possible of those "In what ways might I . . . ?" problem-statements. Avoid the impulse to answer the question; just defer judgment and see how many of these *questions* you can raise.

We'll probably fall between "In what ways might we turn off the faucets," and "In what ways might we filter the water for swimming."

Reprinted by permission of Timi Gleason.

2. Try once more to image the details of the challenge, desire, problem, or idea you are working on. Close your eyes and see how much of the detail (facts or data) you can picture in your imagination.

3. What do you *wish* would happen about what you observed in your imagination? Make as many wishes as you would like, with no concern for restraints or judgment.

4. Convert each wish into "In what ways might I . . . ?" problem-statements.

5. Select the "In what ways might I . . . ?" question you'd like to work on *first;* the one that looks most promising or intriguing; the one for which you'd most like some new ideas now.

6. Try listing synonyms for the verb and other key words in the question.
   EXAMPLE: "What ways might I get rid of the trash?" might become "What ways might I eliminate the trash?" The latter question might prompt ideas for creating less trash in the first place. Changing the verb in a statement of a challenge can help change our mental "set" or out-look regarding the challenge.

7. Finally, choose the words that best express the problem for you and get ready for Idea-Finding.

IDEA-FINDING:

1. Defer judgment and allow your ideas to flow freely without any evaluation at the moment. List, sketch, or symbolize ideas for attacking the problem you just chose. Magnify, minify, and rearrange. Look for obvious analogies as well as strange ones.

2. Try an incubation break — music, relaxation, or some complete change of pace — a refreshment break, exercise, jogging, dancing, etc.

3. Record any new ideas that occurred during or after incubation.

4. Look back at some of your more interesting ideas. *Imagine* each of them as though it existed, as though it were actually taking place. Then try to magnify, minify, and rearrange the idea in your imagination in as many ways as possible; defer judgment and jot down modifications or new ideas that emerge.

5. Choose the idea(s) that look most promising or interesting, and/ or that you *like* best at this time. Remember, if your idea is very general, you may want to consider it as a "sub-problem" and generate specific ideas under it before moving on to the criteria in Solution-Finding.

6. Develop the ideas into a rough plan of action — a kind of tentative statement of what you'd like to do — even if you don't yet know how to work it all out.

SOLUTION-FINDING:

1. List, sketch, or symbolize evaluative criteria to assist you in determining how "good" or "bad" the ideas are. Consider elements which might make them fail, or those which might make them better, and who and what might be affected, etc. Don't forget the "Will it . . . ?" questions.

2. Image others reacting to you as you tell them about your ideas and plan. See their expressions, their "nonverbals." Then add the further criteria that you become aware of.

3. Use the most important criteria as tools to help you tailor your selected "raw" ideas and rough plan into workable ones. Apply deferred judgment and record ways to reshape them to fit the criteria better.

   EXAMPLE: In purchasing a house, a certain couple had included the criterion, "not a corner lot." They found a house that met all their criteria except that one. So they asked themselves, "In what ways might we enjoy the corner lot?" In brainstorming for ideas, they suddenly saw a way to use bushes to provide more privacy than they had formerly enjoyed in their previous house in the middle of the block. At that point they realized that it wasn't the corner lot that was concerning them, but lack of privacy resulting from a corner lot. If the couple had posed the question, "Why are we concerned about a corner lot?" they might have answered, "Because it wouldn't afford the privacy we like." Then they could have restated their problem as, "In what ways might we enjoy privacy on a corner lot?" This might have directed their flow of ideas to the bushes faster than the original question did. It is advisable to "massage" the problem-statement a few times before seeking ideas, whether in Problem-Finding or when we see a new problem emerge in Solution-Finding, as above.

ACCEPTANCE-FINDING:

1. Try a few minutes of relaxation, exercise, change of pace, etc.

2. Now produce a free flow of ideas for gaining acceptance and putting your chosen idea(s) and plan to use. List ways to implement, insure success, improve the original idea(s), show advantages, gain enthusiasm of yourself or others, overcome objections, anticipate possible misconceptions, pretest, etc.

3. Now spell out in *detail* a finalized plan *for the moment.* List as many *specifics* as possible, including first steps you will take, schedule, follow-up, etc. Remember the checklist: *who, what, when, where, why,* and *how.*

4. If you want to generate a great variety of possible plans, try the morphological process described in Chapter 5. Use a *variety* of who's, what's, when's, where's, how's, and why's as the variables to be cross-related.

5. If the idea you want to use is quite difficult to implement, use the "30 Question" checklist in Part III, on page 139. Stretch for as

many ideas as possible under each question. Then select the best ideas to weave into your final plan of action. With extended effort on this, you may achieve major breakthroughs in getting your idea into action.

6. If you are all out of thoughts regarding your plan of action, then do the following . . .

   A. Close your eyes. Relax as fully as you can. Imagine yourself lying in a very comfortable place. Before you is a large TV set. Turn on the TV and see yourself putting your plan into action just as you would like to see it happen. See every detail, every expression and reaction, yours as well as those of others involved.

   B. Now bring into the "picture" an unexpected development. Using your imagination, "watch" the consequences.

   C. Add more ideas to your recorded plan, taking into account what you "saw" and "felt," so that you might further insure the effectiveness of your plan.

   D. Imagine and list new challenges that might result from implementing the plan.

   E. Review in your mind any new connections you can make as a result of the new challenges you just listed. Adapt the details of your plan accordingly. Incubate further on the plan and continue extending your effort toward meeting the challenges that you have been considering, as you put your plan into action. Remember always that "nothing is final!"

I hope you gained some new insights this time. If you didn't, get away from your challenge for a while, incubate. Keep pad and pencil handy to capture ideas. Later on, look over all the thoughts you recorded earlier and during incubation, including other problem-statements or ideas. See whether they suggest new possibilities. Deferring judgment, force new relationships between what you already had and what materialized during incubation. If nothing emerges, try incubation again.

Continue alternating between deliberate involvement and incubation. The probability of a new insight will be greater than by using either process alone. Catch those fleeting thoughts whenever they occur, not just on a "9 to 5" basis.

An interesting example concerns Brahms in his old age. Facing a lengthy period of unproductivity which appeared to be related to the aging process, the musician decided to abandon writing music. When Brahms finally produced his next composition, he explained that having decided not to write anymore "the music came to me without effort."

"I hate to wake him — he might be in the middle of something big."

Reprinted by permission: Tribune Media Services.

CHAPTER TEN

Let's Try Intensive Opportunity-Making!

Being sure that you are fresh and rested again, choose another desire, challenge, concern, or idea that you want to *do* something about. This time you might want to focus on a challenge that I call an "opportunity-type" (implying no urgency) rather than a "concern-type" or "obstacle-type." Some examples might be: planning new ways to use scrap materials or leftover food; a new plan for an office party; or a new way to express your love to your mate. Although you may have successfully dealt with these topics before, the process may help you to discover a whole new realm of value, enjoyment, or satisfaction. Experiencing the joys of creating new and relevant plans in some of these areas will probably motivate you to apply the process in situations where nothing *has* to be done, where no new solutions *have* to be achieved. Here the process becomes great fun in and of itself, and can even provide a new zest for living and working in the plans it generates.

If you decide to go this route in this run-through, one way to sensitize yourself to many "opportunity-type" challenges is to start out by making a cluster of wishes. Have a ball and let the child in you come out. Wish for anything and everything you want; you'll evaluate later. You may be surprised at what you'll generate if you really let go, defer all judgment and let the wishes flow. Even though some may seem ridiculous, the odds are that you'll find one desire that's manageable enough to work on realistically in a half-hour or so.

With whatever wish, dream, or challenge you choose to work on, let's move through the process with just a reminder-summary of each step. If you should need more help in flowing with your thoughts, just go back to the appropriate step in the previous chapters for additional stimuli. If you chose "the big dream," you will need to break it down during the process into many bite-sized pieces. Deal with each element separately over an extended time-period so that you can turn the dream into reality.

FACT-FINDING:

1. List, sketch, or symbolize as many facts and feelings as you can about whatever you have chosen. Who? What? When? Where? Why? How? IMAGE, DEFER JUDGMENT, FLOW!

2. Review what you have written and underscore important elements that suggest problem-statements.

PROBLEM-FINDING:

1. Based on the data arrived at during Fact-Finding, list many questions starting with "In what ways might I . . . (IWWMI)?" Image, wish, ask "why?", find synonyms, etc. Keep recycling your resulting thoughts into new "IWWMI" questions. DEFER JUDGMENT! FLOW!

2. Did you broaden and break down the problem? Now select the problem-statement you like best for creative attack.

IDEA-FINDING:

1. List, sketch, or symbolize many ideas in response to your selected IWWMI question. Magnify, minify, rearrange. Image your ideas. Examine attributes. "Force" relationships. DEFER JUDGMENT, FLOW!

2. Choose the idea(s) you want to use first.

SOLUTION-FINDING:

1. List, sketch, or symbolize many evaluative criteria: Effects on . . . Will it . . . ? Image, empathize. DEFER JUDGMENT! FLOW!

2. Glance over the criteria you recorded, underscoring those that you find especially important.

ACCEPTANCE-FINDING:

1. Use the criteria as tools to help you tailor your raw ideas into workable solutions. List, sketch, or symbolize many ideas to help

"... It's not a parking space if you can't open the doors ..."

meet the challenges suggested by the criteria. Improve ideas, reshape, modify, adapt, magnify, minify, rearrange, combine, substitute. Fantasize! List many who's, what's, where's, when's, why's, how's for gaining acceptance and implementing your ideas. DEFER JUDGMENT! FLOW!

2. Now spell out a detailed plan. Image it taking place. Record new challenges of which you became aware and ways of dealing with these challenges. If the idea is quite difficult to implement, try the "30 Questions" checklist on page 139 (Part III). Continue alternating with incubation.

Are You Going With The Probabilities?

Usually by applying the five-step process we break through to something worthwhile regarding our challenge or problem. When the "30 Questions" are used for additional flow in the Acceptance-Finding step, the probabilities of arriving at something worthwhile are increased significantly. By alternating incubation with deliberate effort, the probabilities are increased even more. An *aha* is never guaranteed, but each time we allow for one more thought our chance of success is more probable.

Keep reviewing your earlier lists of thoughts on the challenge or problem. Then in light of your current awareness, see whether you can make some new connections to those earlier thoughts, so as to modify or transform them into helpful improvements for your plan.

And the more you are willing and able to defer your decision while going through these processes, the greater the *probability* of a breakthrough to a better plan of action.

Are You Chipping Away?

The nature of the creative person can be dramatized by the story of the little boy who saw a sculptor beginning to work on a solid granite block. As he went by each day on his way to school, he paid little attention to the sculptor chipping away at the block. Then one day he suddenly noticed the emerging shape of a fully formed lion. "How did you know *it* was in there?" he asked the sculptor. The person working creatively "knows" a solution is there, and is willing to keep chipping away bit by bit until that solution emerges.

Michelangelo, while examining a piece of marble, reputedly said, "There is an angel imprisoned in it and I must set it free." We might say, "There is a solution frozen up in our minds, and we must melt it down and let it flow out." The procedures you have been exposed to in this book are designed to help that happen. Sometimes they help the problem itself melt away.

"I THINK YOU SHOULD BE MORE EXPLICIT HERE IN STEP TWO."

© 1996 by Sidney Harris.

CHAPTER ELEVEN

All Set For Solo Flight?

Now, how about trying the process all by yourself? Prepare six sheets of paper with the following headings: 1. Fact-Finding (Data, including feelings); 2. Problem-Finding ("In what ways might I . . ." definitions); 3. Idea-Finding (Ideas); 4. Solution-Finding (Criteria — Improvements); 5. Acceptance-Finding (Implementation-ideas); 6. Plan of Action (including new challenges to be handled). Choose a new desire, challenge, concern, or idea, or something from your lists in Chapter 8 or 10.

Too often we deal only with problems that are blatantly in our way. An inordinate amount of time is spent "putting out fires" rather than structuring our lives so that fewer fires occur. We often cope in the sense of "I have to put up with it" instead of coping by imaging, dreaming, or foreseeing, and then dealing constructively with the vision. We allow ourselves to be controlled by our environment rather than being the controllers. We *re*-act rather than *pro*-act. We can create the problems, the mysteries, then solve them; or we can act only in the role of a detective, forever solving the mysteries or problems with which someone else confronts us.

If you are confronted by a pressing problem, then go with it and search for new ways of viewing and responding to it. Later perhaps you can try more of the "pro-acting" variety.

On the other hand, you might try for a challenge that you only sense or anticipate now. List a few like that, perhaps "wishes" that pop to mind, or use the first ten of the prompters again on page 73, number 2 to trigger a few additional ones. Then zero in on the one you'd like to use for this "solo" run-through.

Whatever the case, make your choice and go right on to Fact-Finding on your first page; then continue through your Plan of Action page.

Perhaps your plan of action will only be a first step — "a juggling of one orange." But, it can start a momentum that can grow and develop as you do more and more with additional ideas later. So, be sure to schedule into your plan a time to review the other thoughts you recorded. You may then "chip away," bit-by-bit, the broader issues involved.

You might appreciate the touching reaction I once received to the "blank-page" type of session you just experienced in this chapter. It was from a partially-deaf student. Asked what she had gained from the session, she wrote, "Insight of what life is all about and that life to each individual is a blank page which only he can through experience fill; mostly he does it alone."

Our Drive For Ideas

It might be well to emphasize the relationship between learning creative problem-solving and learning to drive a car. When people first learn to drive, they are very conscious of each movement that is made with their hands and feet. After they have driven for a while, the movements become automatic — almost subconscious.

In working through this book, you have been learning to make certain "thinking movements" quite deliberately. Later you will probably find them to be subconscious — almost automatic. It will be as though you automatically make *new* connections and derive *ahas* in your problem-sensing and solving, not only by chance when "sleeping on it," but also when actively pursuing it mentally.

Let us extend the automobile analogy. When we first experience the full use of the process as in Chapter 8, it may be comparable to the first use of freeways in traveling cross-country. The super-highways provided unrestricted flow for long expanses, but then ended at large cities. We had to slow down to a snail's pace as we wound our way through city traffic. Likewise as you converged in the process at the end of each step, you may have found it very confining or frustrating to "slow down." Continuing the analogy, we now have city by-passes as part of our freeway system. We slow down only somewhat as we meet greater traffic around the city. Similarly, as you become more and more familiar and comfortable with the process, you learn to build your own "by-passes" and need slow down only slightly as you go from one step to another. The entire process then becomes smoother and more natural or comfortable, including your moving back and forth from deliberate to incubative effort.

CHAPTER TWELVE

Let's Really Emphasize Speed Thinking!

Let's speed up the process until it becomes internalized. We'll practice on some simple challenges like, "I'd enjoy concocting a new soup," or "I'd like to make the people at work feel good tomorrow." The following checklist may help trigger a variety of such challenges for you:

Family	Nutrition
Friends	Energy
Neighbors	Politics
Church	Health
Home	Recreation
Work	Purchases
Hobbies	Resources
Education	Finances
Transportation	Communication
Social Life	Technology
Sex	Aesthetics
Relationships	Retirement

Choose *one* of those you thought of.

Now, considering the challenge you selected, try spending *only a few minutes* on each step below.

FACT-FINDING:

1. Record the facts and feelings of the situation.

2. Image them as fully as you can; focus on the most significant.

PROBLEM-FINDING:

1. Record the "In What Ways Might I . . . (IWWMI)?" statements that come to mind. Keep rephrasing more IWWMI's as a result of answering "why?"

2. Choose the statement that best reflects what you would like to accomplish at this moment. (Some statements may be good for later, more lengthy attacks.) Then fantasize accomplishing it, by magic if necessary.

IDEA-FINDING:

1. Record ideas as fast as possible, using every technique you know, including imaging, magnifying, minifying, rearranging, etc.

2. Select the idea(s) that intrigue you, the one(s) you like best.

SOLUTION -FINDING:

1. Record as many criteria as possible from as many different viewpoints as possible. Imagine yourself in others' skins.

2. Focus on the criteria you feel are most important, considering your own attitudes as well as those of others involved. Start improving your idea to make it more workable, more manageable with respect to the criteria.

ACCEPTANCE-FINDING:

1. Record as many ways as possible to make your idea(s) work, to gain mutual acceptance, to get action. Image your ideas and keep revising them to meet the needs of your criteria, to add strength, to make the ideas more interesting or fun, etc.

2. Select your best implementation-ideas to work into a specific plan of action. What will be your first step within the next 24 hours? . . . What next? . . . Where? . . . How? . . . With whom? . . . Why? . . . Image it happening.

HERMAN © Jim Unger.
Reprinted with permission of
UNIVERSAL PRESS SYNDICATE.
All rights reserved.

Action Plan:

Do you have a plan that you feel good about? If not, try a bit of incubation. Then look back at your notes and see if anything new pops out. Repeat until you make some new connections that please you.

Try the process on several more "opportunity-type" challenges until you feel comfortable with the process and experience positive results more and more quickly. Once you are experiencing success, try compressing the process into less time for each step until you are doing the entire process in several minutes. Be sure to generate at least two or three thoughts under each step rather than merely the first thought.

Now try the same rapid process on an "obstacle-type" challenge like "I forgot to bring something home that my _____ is expecting" or "My secretary just handed me this poorly-typed letter that must be mailed today and he/she is ready to leave for the day." Make them *simple* challenges that need a decision quickly. Although they may not be earth-shaking, they can certainly make a difference. List some of these.

Select one of the challenges you listed and follow the same procedure as outlined on the previous pages. Limit yourself to a few minutes per step:
- Fact-Finding
- Problem-Finding
- Idea-Finding
- Solution-Finding
- Acceptance-Finding
- Plan of Action

Now, choose another challenge from your list and try the process again. Reduce the time you spend on each step. Do this gradually until you are doing the entire process in a minute or so, with several thoughts flowing under each step rather than only the first impulse or "habit-thought." If you like, do it totally in your head without any writing.

Prove to yourself that you can do the entire process in a very short time when necessary; many problems in daily living have such time constraints. But, when the situation warrants it, you can profit by spending long blocks of time flowing with large numbers of thoughts under each step. You be the judge as to how much time you should spend in each situation. Remember, you can extend your effectiveness by allowing incubation periods as much as possible before making final decisions. Work back and forth *between* challenges, letting incubation take over when you remove your conscious attention. When you do so you increase the likelihood that an important element buried in your memory may surface to your consciousness. Be prepared always to capture it.

Dr. Lawrence Kubie, in his book, *Neurotic Distortion Of The Creative Process,* tells of research where individuals were placed in a strange room for a few minutes. After they left the room, they were asked to list all the items they had seen there. The average person listed 20-30 items. After being placed under hypnosis, however, the same individuals then listed an average of about 200 more items!

Each of us has a deep well of knowledge buried in our mind; creative problem-solving involves many diverse processes — beyond incubation alone — to tap it and apply it to our present concerns.

You probably know the five steps by heart now: Fact-Finding, Problem-Finding, Idea-Finding, Solution-Finding, Acceptance-Finding. As a final challenge, you might want to walk through the process mentally in just a minute's time. Defer your immediate, impulsive, habitual, "prejudiced" response to a situation until you take a few moments to form new associations — to seek new viewpoints. You always have your habit response to fall back on, but chances are that you will discover some new element in one of the five steps that may make your response more effective.

Practice and more practice will enable you to change the habit of *re*-acting to something, to one of *pro*-acting. Whether deferring just long enough to make a snap decision without falling into the habit trap, or spending hours flowing through the process when appropriate, you are more likely to make a successful decision — while at the same time conditioning yourself to be always more comfortable and capable in meeting any new situation. Thus you develop increasing confidence that you can handle successfully *whatever* comes up in your life and work.

In creative problem-solving we capitalize on the deepest feasible search of the past as the springboard for a creative leap into the future. We strive to bring an ever greater amount of knowledge into working consciousness and interpolate it into projections of what might be. We then test these projections mentally. If and as our careful evaluation and development warrant, we then implement our new future.

Our Unbeatable Mind!

You may have read of the American prisoner-of-war who maintained his sanity during years of captivity and torture by deliberately exercising his imagination. He pictured himself building the dream house he wanted — room-by-room, brick-by-brick, nail-by-nail — until he had designed and built every square inch of the house in his mind. If, when being tortured, he lost the mental vision, he would begin all over again. His mind prevailed, and on his return to the United States, he built the dream house he had conceived.

Our mind can be our most powerful possession. It can discover our most exciting challenges, solve our toughest problems, and serve us when all else may seem to have failed. Don't ever lose sight of the magic of your mind!

TYRANTS HAVE NOT YET
DISCOVERED ANY CHAINS
THAT CAN FETTER THE MIND.
... COLTON

CHAPTER THIRTEEN

Introduction To Part III:
What Makes An
Effective Facilitator?

I use the term "facilitator" to identify the leader who *draws out, reinforces, and thus facilitates the creative learning, development, and problem solving of the people with whom he or she is working. The person facilitating creative behavior is aware of the creative process and first understands it in himself or herself, and then is able to help others see and strengthen it in themselves.* If one does not understand this, the facilitator may only frustrate another when the latter sees the creative behavior of the first person but doesn't know how to achieve it.

The following explains *my* conception of an effective facilitator. He or she believes in the capability of people to be creative beings, is open to ideas and viewpoints, prone to question rather than tell, "Socratic" in stance as well as "deferjudicing." ("Deferjudicing" is a term I used in Part II to connote the desire and ability to take ever-increasing amounts of data into consideration, *in a given unit of time,* before reaching a decision. This is contrasted with the two extremes of prejudice and indecisiveness.)

Enthusiasm is helpful in a facilitator but there can be a kind of self-evident sincerity, not necessarily the bubbly type of enthusiasm. Other qualities of an effective facilitator could include a sense of humor, a fondness or acceptance of all kinds of people, quick thinking, the ability to use the creative process rapidly, and the ability to live happily in ambiguity, not just to tolerate it. The facilitator *invites* ambiguity — yet can maintain the balance necessary for using the creative process to bring a greater order from the disorder in the ambiguity. The person *looks* for something positive in a circumstance, idea, person or a thing, and is tactful. The ideal facilitator can remain on the sidelines — doesn't need the "spotlight;" is kind and concerned, optimistic; laughs or smiles a lot; doesn't take self too seriously; is interested in others; is a hard worker — self-motivated, sincere, dedicated, confident that the creative process will carry one through; is willing to take calculated risks where one's own efforts may make a difference; is spontaneous, flexible, accepting; can get a group to cohere; has "group-building" ability; is aware of nonverbal clues or feelings; respects the potential of individuals and the group as a whole; makes fun out of the process at times — tolerates some foolishness — but always works toward a serious objective; plays hunches; is conscious of time constraints, but is flexible within them.

The more the facilitator knows about the problem-area being considered, the more effective he or she can be. Although a good facilitator can operate without complete content-expertise, he or she can apply the creative process to finding information and helping members of a problem-solving group do so, too.

Facilitating the creative process primarily involves removing the blocks to creative functioning and accelerating the process where possible. It might be said that the psychological blocks hindering creative behavior are both internal and external. It behooves the leader to establish a kind of climate providing for what Carl Rogers calls "psychological freedom" and "psychological safety." The participants are helped to feel at ease, to explore, play, experiment, and fail, in the early stages of each step of the process. However, there is full understanding that deferring of judgment during these periods of spontaneity and experimentation will be followed by significant analysis, development, evaluation, and synthesis. They not only feel psychologically safe and free, but confident that their efforts will produce significant results and will be followed to a valid conclusion and action.

In considering the skill development in a facilitator, I offer the following analogy. Probably no athlete is *many times* taller, faster, or stronger than others. However, most athletes are much more *effective in using* an innate physical characteristic than the average person. They have become so by strenuously cultivating a somewhat greater advantage that they already possessed. If a person has the potential for being a good facilitator, then by intensive practice the individual might become just as skillful in leading an effective problem-solving session as an Olympic athlete might be in a developed skill.

A facilitator might also be likened to an orchestra conductor who needs *constant* practice. Leopold Stokowski once reported that if he didn't rehearse for one day, he knew it. If he didn't rehearse for two days, the critics knew it, and if he didn't rehearse for three days, the audience knew it. The facilitator likewise needs constant practice to maintain a high level of skill.

You are a creative artist when you are facilitating. Your medium consists of the talents in the group you are leading. As former U.S. Defense Secretary Robert McNamara once said, *"Management is, in the end, the most creative of all the arts, for its medium is human talent itself."* Each session can be a new creative product, just like each painting is a new creation for the artist.

Again, one might view the deliberate development of creative behavior as an exaggerated push for change. We "stretch" people beyond their normal limits in an oscillating process of imagining and judging during all stages of problem solving — in piling up facts, defining viewpoints of the problem, generating ideas, recognizing criteria, and finding ways to insure the successful acceptance and implementation of ideas. That is how we provide practice in intensive stretching between conception and action. The result has been scientifically demonstrated as increasing ability to consider many more factors in a given time in making decisions.

As facilitators practice this type of leadership with more and more varied groups, they become conditioned to these processes and become able to take increasing numbers of factors into consideration in a given time in making decisions. Hence, the facilitator becomes a highly creative leader. If we could expose all our nation's leaders to these processes, to draw upon the creativity dormant in all groups and individuals, it might make a world of difference in how they handle problems of state.

CHAPTER FOURTEEN

How Do We Facilitate The Process?

The following thoughts occurred to me over the years during reflection about the facilitator's function in a variety of groups. I consider the suggestions significant but embryonic in terms of what we will learn about this little-discussed area of "facilitation" in the sense that we are using it. Although there are definite relationships in the facilitating process we are discussing to the whole field of group dynamics and interpersonal-behavior programs, we are dealing with something more specific — leadership of a *deferred judgment* session. That is the unique part of our consideration. The qualities required when judgments and decisions are made in different stages of the creative problem-solving process are general leadership qualities required for good group dynamics. The suggestions emphasized here generally relate to encouraging a free flow of thoughts while groups defer judgment, and then helping participants move toward convergence.

A Note Of Caution

In the suggestions that follow, I will list general ones first, then specific ones in each stage of the CPS process. Generally I'll list ideas which have worked well for me. But, in *particular* circumstances they may be ineffective or counterproductive. Assess each facilitating situation on its own merits and use the suggestions where they seem to fit. If a suggestion doesn't make sense or is uncomfortable for you, don't use it. Or, adapt it to fit the situation.

Each time I reread the manuscript during its preparation, I changed, added, or deleted something. I will never be satisfied because I am continually learning about this skill that is probably a science as well as an art. However, people have frequently asked me to write about the specific behaviors I exhibit during facilitation. This has prompted me to try to pinpoint ways I *seem* to function best in that role. I offer all my suggestions only in that vein. They are not "rules."

My suggestions assume a working knowledge of the CPS process as provided in Parts I and II. Sometimes a suggestion may not be clear to someone without that or similar background.

The term "client" is used in some of the suggestions that follow. This is the party responsible for decision and action regarding a problem or challenge. It may be a member of the group being facilitated through the process, or it may be the group itself if working on a common problem for which it has group responsibility for decision and action.

General Suggestions

1. Provide lots of flip-chart paper to quickly record ideas so the group can use them in subsequent stages. Keep the recordings in front of the group at all times for constant stimulation and reference. Label each step at the top of each sheet. Number the items for easy reference — and challenge the group by always listing several additional numbers.

2. Have a watch available for checking time as you move through the session.

3. Have pads and pencils for each participant; encourage each to jot down any thoughts they cannot get onto the flip-charts because of speed of flow. Pick these up later during a lull or just before the convergent stage of any step.

4. Remember that your attitude, manner, facial expressions, body movements, and words will tell the group a lot regarding your openness and receptivity to *all* its thoughts.

5. Develop informality. For example, at times have everyone, if comfortable doing so, sit on the floor with a piece of flip-chart paper in the center of the group and with everyone writing down contributions. This provides an opportunity for fast recording, interaction, and thought-connecting.

6. Vary the pace by oscillating between group, subgroup, dyad activity, and individual listing of thoughts. If working on a "client" problem, keep the group actively involved in all deferred-judgment phases and as actively or constructively as possible when the client is converging, selecting, or deciding. Give the rest of the group a short break if a convergent stage becomes lengthy, unless participants are actively involved helping the client by making judgments and giving them to the client for consideration.

"ALTHOUGH HUMANS MAKE SOUNDS WITH THEIR MOUTHS AND OCCASIONALLY LOOK AT EACH OTHER, THERE IS NO SOLID EVIDENCE THAT THEY ACTUALLY COMMUNICATE WITH EACH OTHER."

© 1996 Sidney Harris

7. Actively listen and observe the group and its personality interactions. Watch for nonverbal indications of dissatisfaction with your recording summary. After a flurry of recording and "short-handing" of statements, ask the group to determine if you missed or misinterpreted anything.

8. If contributions are coming quickly, your biggest problem may be to keep from interrupting. You may have many contributions of your own, but will need to hold back to further encourage the group. Most of your leadership skills can be used to monitor the process, perhaps raising leading, *open-ended* questions if discussion might better move in a different direction. For example: Fact-Finding — *What additional kinds of information might we obtain?* Problem-Finding — *What other definitions might there be?* Idea-Finding — *In what ways might we get more of such and such?* Solution-Finding — *What other people might be affected?* Acceptance-Finding — *What other times and places might add impact?*

9. One of my favorite edicts is *"If in doubt, leave it out,"* whenever I'm trying to decide if I should interrupt — which I really want to avoid.

10. Keep relevance in mind as your ultimate objective. If you don't know if you're on the right track, or you're not sure what's happening, ask yourself *"Where are we heading?"; "What is our ultimate objective in this step or in the total session?"* Then re-orient yourself based on your answer. Take advantage of periods of individual, dyad or subgroup writing for this thinking.

11. Be genuine. Don't pretend; don't hesitate to tell the group you don't know, you're not sure or you're not clear. Participants may be expecting a familiar style of autocratic or "know-it-all" leadership or "teaching." Your candor in not being the infallible expert will be refreshing and will probably help open the group members up to their own potentials.

12. Listen carefully to show your openness and interest. With complex or critical contributions, use reflective listening techniques, where you paraphrase what you have heard. Check back to see if you've understood it correctly.

13. Vary the session by having members move around the room for a moment or two. You might place many sheets of paper on the walls and have participants jot ideas randomly on different sheets.

14. Try for spurts in every stage of the process. Don't let the deferred-judgment session become a discussion rather than a free, spontaneous flow of thoughts.

15. Set quotas and deadlines to spur the group. During the convergent phase, point out instances when they selected late thoughts on the list.

16. Encourage use of imagery any time in the process, particularly where an increased flow or more originality is needed.

17. Try to say nothing negative. Turn negative reactions into positives. If someone misinterprets a step and gives ideas during Fact-Finding, capture the thoughts and try to turn them into what the group is seeking at the time. If that confuses the group, stop the process and constructively point out the nature of the particular step and the emphasis sought, or rephrase the step's introduction. For example, in Fact-Finding ask, *"What other information might we like to have?"* or *"What other data are available?"* The entry point to any step is usually a question to promote flow. This question can be used again and again, as necessary, for re-emphasis or to re-capture the group's attention to the focus of the particular step.

18. Use humility and a sense of humor — don't be afraid to plead or beg, in a kidding way, for "another 10 ideas."

19. Use expressions like, *"If you'll bear with me"; "How about trying . . . ?"; "Would you mind if we did such and so?"; "Would you be willing to try a brief experiment?";* or *"If we could take the next so much time for such and so, I think I might be able to illustrate something through your own experience."* Avoid commanding — *"Do this," "Make a list of," "I want you to . . ."*

20. Use words like *"trigger"* and *"flow"* to emphasize what you are seeking.

21. Don't be afraid to interject a thought of your own but do so casually, as merely another contribution. Do not push your view. If you are getting more thoughts than you can handle, jot some down while asking everyone to record individually. These contributions can be added to the input or given to the client for later consideration.

22. Keep trying to speed recording when the ideas come fast by adding an extra recorder or by having people write their ideas on multiple sheets, or stick-on notes to then attach to the sheets.

23. Ask the group's help when you need it. Don't be afraid to say, *"I can't figure out what's happening here, why we're tending to bog down; can anyone help me?"* When one member begins to argue with you or criticize the process, avoid a debate or a direct response. Try to get the group to give its reactions to what is happening and how members feel about the situation. See if the group can clarify your

points if someone does not understand. One of the worst things a facilitator can do is argue with a participant or with the group. Count on the reasonableness and logic of the group as a whole. Generally, that will help. During this kind of episode, if you are trying to get others to respond and people keep looking to you as they talk or question, look around the group. Try to divert the contributor's eyes from yours so they may start looking at other people and getting more interaction from them.

24. If anything tends to become a continuing dialogue between two people, pass an object back and forth, between yourself and another person, and show what happens to group interest and involvement compared with shooting the object — basketball style — from one to an unexpected other around the room. This illustrates the dynamics of real *group* interaction around a question.

25. As time runs out for any step, have the participants write their last thoughts and put them up in front of the room. When discussing a client's problem, let the group pass its thoughts directly to the client.

26. Emphasize time limits tactfully, or even kiddingly, as you "force" the group to conclude, even if members don't feel they are finished. Make the point that our lives are governed by deadlines. (Death is our ultimate deadline.)

27. At any convergent step, ask yourself whether the group needs to reach a consensus. If not, let the client decide, or an individual or subgroup — whatever system makes sense to move the group comfortably and realistically into the next step.

28. Try to merge all the session's events toward your ultimate end — a viable action plan. Tie them in like Duke Ellington did with the airplane flying above the stadium where he was playing. He conducted the sound of the plane along with the orchestra. This technique becomes a facilitator's constant creative challenge.

29. When facilitating, you are concentrating on the process more than anyone else in the group. If everyone were concentrating on the process, there would be less need for a facilitator. Since this is rarely the case, the facilitator must continually monitor the process, breaking roadblocks and speeding activity.

30. If you tend to get so absorbed in content that you forget the process yourself, you should avoid participating in the content area. This is especially true when you are facilitating your own problem.

31. The "why" question is applicable in several ways. In Fact-Finding it can be a key question to bring out data — for example,

"Why might this be happening?" In Problem-Finding it can help redefine the problem, as explained in the later Problem-Finding section. In Acceptance-Finding it can be another key question — for example, *"Why might they want to help?"* Even in Solution-Finding, if it is fully understood, the "why" question can be used skillfully to reach specific aspects of major criteria such as cost. *"Why might cost be a criterion?"* Answers: *"Because we want to reduce waste"* or *"Because time is money."* Each could then be translated into another criterion, such as "waste it would incur," "time it would take."

The thing to avoid in asking "why?" is doing it in an accusatory way. People are accustomed to being asked "why?" as a challenge to what they have just said. They believe they must defend themselves. That is not how to use "why" in the facilitating process. If it is used properly, it can stimulate more flow.

32. As a facilitator *you* are judging — not a specific thought, but the general nature of the flow — to make decisions during all deferred-judgment phases. If this were not so, the group might go on forever in any step and might be less productive than with a facilitator guiding it.

33. Don't forget the power of incubation. Take advantage of any breaks, including refreshment, lunch, overnight or even after the work on the problem is "completed." Emphasize "sleeping on it" and preparing for revisions the next morning as a result of incubated thoughts. Urge members to use all the time available until the idea must be put into effect, to make additions or improvements. Encourage members to keep reviewing the earlier thoughts on all the sheets as they move into the process' final stages, to see how the first thoughts may modify or support later ones.

34. Learn to co-facilitate effectively when the opportunity arises. If more than one facilitator is available, don't treat it as an opportunity to divide the "on stage" time in half. Learn to work as a team. The one taking a more active role at any moment can be monitored and supported by the other, who constructively questions, injects thoughts or brings ideas up in effective pre-planned ways. This greatly increases the power of facilitation. Effective teams may try to create a kind of kidding, funlike cooperation in facilitation which the group may begin to emulate.

35. If the group's productivity is poor and you can't raise the productivity level, take a "process break" and tell the group what you're noticing and feeling. Try to clear up the difficulties and return the group to a higher production level. One leader, Gil Rapaille, assigned an ob-

server to count the number of ideas per minute in a group's Idea-Finding phase. When the level went below a critical number, the observer told the leader, who stopped the session for the "process break."

36. Lack of productivity can be observed in the form of low energy. The ideas may be coming, but they are not producing "ahas" and the kind of group involvement we are seeking. The energy and productivity levels usually mirror group commitment and involvement. When the facilitator cannot feel the group's energy, commitment, interest or involvement in other than a perfunctory way, he or she has an indication that the process is not working. Specific ways can be used to assess this commitment, such as, are they getting excited? — are they leaning forward? — are they laughing "with" shared newness and strangeness?

Moving Into The Actual Process

As you begin facilitating the specific steps of the process, there are things you can do to help maximize the results of each particular step. I have found the following suggestions especially helpful in the steps indicated, although many of the ideas may have relevance elsewhere as well. The creative facilitator will make adaptations and applications in a variety of circumstances throughout the process.

OBJECTIVE-FINDING (MESS OR OBJECTIVE):

1. When referring to the "mess" we begin with, refrain from using the word "problem." Stress that we do not dignify it with the word "problem" at that point, reserving the term until the problem-finding step. Many facilitators use "objective-finding," which adds a prestep to the five-step process and provides the acronym, OFPISA (Objective, Fact, Problem, Idea, Solution, Acceptance) popularized by the late Bert J. Decker. In a sense, we refer to the situation or the mess as equivalent to Decker's "objective." It is the situation we are seeking to improve.

2. Move into "objective-finding" or "mess-finding" with questions like *"What kinds of desires, challenges, opportunities, or concerns do you have in your life?"* By avoiding the word "problem" here you may encourage flow rather than have people trying prematurely to define precisely. Of course, if you begin the session with a given "problem" (mess or objective), then move directly into Fact-Finding.

3. Point out that often the only difference between an "obstacle" and an "opportunity" is the way it is expressed. For example, *"This room is dismal"* vs. *"Hey, let's brighten up this room."*

"I <u>do</u> think your problems are serious, Richard.
They're just not very interesting."

Drawing by Koren; © 1974
The New Yorker Magazine, Inc.

4. When the facilitator desires to stretch the group for more relevant and interesting objectives, particularly if these are not forthcoming in the early offerings, refer to the checklist below, excerpted from my book *Visionizing*.

Eliciting 'Messes' or Objectives: The following is a checklist of "stimulators." List challenges or objectives you think of as you read the stimulators. As you consider each word in the *left* column, apply to it one or more of the words in the *right* column. For example, the word "house" in the left column, when related to the word "complications" in the right column, might suggest the challenge, *"How to speed up the amortization of my mortgage."* "Car" and "waste" might suggest *"How to get into a car pool."*

Friends?	Improvements?
Family?	Happiness and comfort?
Neighbors?	Misunderstandings?
Church?	Complications?
House?	Waste or inefficiencies?
School?	Bottlenecks and routines?
Job responsibilities?	Attitudes?
Promotion?	Anxieties or fears?
Car or transportation?	Anger or disgust?
Social life?	Pet peeves and complaints?
Personality?	Safety?
Hobbies and leisure time?	Economy?
Finances?	Performance?
Plans and goals?	Durability?
Hopes and desires?	Appearance?
Career?	Popularity?

5. Another way to increase the probability of eliciting some engaging messes or objectives is to ask people to make "wish" or "dream" lists. Each is a potential objective.

6. When using the checklist in number 4, or "wishes," or the imagery approaches below, it is usually helpful to urge people to write down everything coming to mind and to emphasize they will only share what they *wish* to share later. This tends to free their minds of concern and judgment, especially if they start thinking of personal matters. After they have developed an extensive list, they can choose items they feel comfortable sharing with the group.

7. Elicit *feelings* so people become more involved. A cartoon dramatically illustrated the importance of involvement or "ownership" of a problem. The wife had the husband turn on the water in the kitchen sink. When he turned the knob, water splashed him in the face. The wife exclaimed, "There, *that's* what's the matter with it!" Try to have the other person "experience" the problem!

8. Imagery processes are especially effective in this phase. Have participants imaginatively re-live a day in their lives and then jot down opportunities or concerns observed or felt during the experience.

9. Don't worry about how the "mess" or objective is worded. Avoid getting analytical. We are looking for a "headline" — something to help focus the person's concern.

10. With a good list of possibilities, there will probably be several items of interest to the group. The selected item might be a particular client's concern or it might be a group concern or perhaps a concern of several group members. It is important that *all* members are willing and committed to work constructively on the mess or objective in order for the session to be productive. This can be the case even if the problem is not important to everyone in the group. In this case, each member needs to be intrigued by the session's focus or be concerned enough about the individual or individuals to help them resolve the problem.

11. Often when one person selects a concern, another has the immediate answer and begins to "lecture" about a possible solution. This can be treated like a Synectics® purge. That is, if the person really has something that immediately satisfies the "client," that may be all there is to it. In most cases, however, it will not do so and may just serve as additional input into Fact-Finding. Often whatever is said can be treated as additional data the person can consider as one begins to focus on what is known about the situation.

12. In selecting the mess or objective, the most significant criteria are usually: (1) the significance of the question to the individual involved, (2) the willingness and/or commitment of the group to work productively on it and (3) the likelihood that something productive can be accomplished. If the situation is a broad generalization, the focus may come during Fact-Finding or Problem-Finding. You will begin to narrow down the problem within the session's time constraint. Therefore, almost anything can be dealt with as a mess or objective if the individual and group have a commitment and interest in it and will accept "ownership" of it. We may actually zero in on some small

aspect of it in Problem-Finding. In this case, Fact-Finding might be superficial until a specific subproblem is developed. At that stage we might re-enter Fact-Finding to examine the subproblem.

FACT-FINDING:

1. Fact-Finding is an elaboration of the mess or objective. We are beginning to observe more about the mess as it was given. Therefore, there can be a natural flow from the original statement of the objective into and through Fact-Finding. To heighten the process you might ask, *"What do we know about this situation?" "What is and isn't happening?" "Who is and isn't involved?" "Where and when is and isn't this taking place?" "How and why is and isn't it happening?"* The focus here is on "is" and "does" — what *exists* — what is currently happening — not what *might be*. It is descriptive, photographic. "Paint a picture" of the mess or objective, including feelings and emotions. Flow of thoughts can be prompted by having participants image the situation as vividly as possible.

2. In Fact-Finding the objective is to gain as clear a picture of the situation as possible. How far to go with this stage depends on the situation and the time available.

3. If someone is describing a "studying" problem and one participant mentions in Fact-Finding that "you're not trying hard enough," the "fact" can be written on the flip-chart as "So and so thinks John is not trying hard enough," and the group can proceed to the next fact. As long as the instructor makes sure the facts are not misinterpreted and emphasizes that an opinion is a fact to the person who holds it, the free-wheeling atmosphere of Fact-Finding can be maintained without debate.

Use all the senses and feelings and don't ignore opinions and attitudes. Treat them as givens in a situation. If a person "feels this way," that is a fact. We don't have to agree with it, but by accepting and acknowledging feelings, opinions and attitudes openly, without argument or criticism, people will tend to relax, open up and let the facts pour out.

4. During Fact-Finding it is useful not only to gather all possible data, but to raise all the data-finding questions which might need answering, which answers are then sought. In fact, the group can be creative by discovering new ways to gather data rather than using only the obvious. This can be very productive in an effective resolution

of the mess or objective. Thus, the key creative challenge in Problem-Finding frequently becomes, *"In What Ways Might I find out . . . ?"* In that case, ideas are next sought on alternative ways to uncover desired data.

5. Be careful using the word "how" — so it doesn't trigger Problem-Finding statements or ideas instead of *"How is it happening?"* or *"How is it not happening?"* When people hear "how," they often jump to *"How might it happen?"* Therefore, it can be effective to ask "How?" at the end of the question sequence so that if this happens, you can move directly into Problem-Finding.

6. To know when to move to Problem-Finding, determine if the group understands enough about the situation to deal constructively with it. There is often an advantage at this point in members not knowing so much that understanding tends to put in too many constraints. However, if the group doesn't know enough to understand what the client is talking about, that is a signal that more Fact-Finding is necessary. A second test of whether Fact-Finding has been productive is to find out if the client or group received any new insights into the situation. Did some facts suggest forgotten aspects of the situation or aspects out of awareness when the group started to focus on the mess or objective?

If the group is not seeing any new light in the situation and if there is time, it can be valuable to "push" viewing the situation in strange ways. For example, participants may be given peanuts and asked to look for aspects of the object reminding them of things about the situation they are examining. In the case of the peanut, is there a shell involved in the mess, in the situation? What might the shell represent?

7. The convergence in the Fact-Finding step can be a circling or connecting of key elements among the listed facts. If the list is short, it may be just a reviewing and "burning into our minds" of the "picture" which has been developed.

PROBLEM-FINDING:

1. The best way I know to move into Problem-Finding quickly and productively is by asking for *"In what ways might I or we"* (IWWMI) questions — perhaps pointing out that *"How might I?"* (or we) is just as reasonable, but does not emphasize quantity as well. Both connote the forward-thrusting, "ownership," action-oriented, infinite-possibility stance desired in the problem statements to be listed.

2. If the IWWMI statements are coming well, wait a few minutes before trying to introduce processes like the "why" question. (Number 4 below.)

3. Deeper thought might be stimulated with the "wish." *"What do you wish would happen?"* — then change each wish into a *"what ways might I?"* problem-statement. Imagery can be helpful here. Image the wish fulfilled even if fancifully, as if by moving a magic wand? See if new IWWMI's are suggested by images obtained.

Sometimes people make wishes such as, "I wish this person were still alive." Here the facilitator might urge rephrasings such as, *"In what way might I make my life feel like that person is still alive?"* — or different interpretations that might lead to challenging problem statements.

4. Generally, if people do not redefine the problem in a broadening way during spontaneous flow, the "Why?" can be introduced after there has been a good list of problem-statements — or even as a "massaging" of the problem-statement selected when converging from the free-flow list. It may also be worth emphasizing that the "why?" can develop subproblems as well as helping broaden the problem. For example, *"Why?"* might broaden *"In what ways might I improve the outdoor grill?"* to *"How to enjoy eating outdoors?"* Or it might lead to a subproblem such as, *"How to keep the smoke from getting to us?"* or *"How to make the grill easy to clean?"* Both directions can be explored both up and down the levels of abstraction or generalization of the problem. Another variation of "Why?" is *"In order to what?"* — *"Towards what objective?"* — *"What do I really want to accomplish?"*

5. When the "Why?" question brings subproblems instead of broader statements, these are often causes of the problem. Therefore, another way to get at subproblems is to ask, *"What are some causes of this problem?"* Many will be implicit in the facts. Therefore, looking back at the facts can help stimulate Problem-Finding questions, reworded as IWWMI.

6. Sometimes the group finds itself repeating things from Fact-Finding by simply rewording them as problems. For example, a listed *fact is "people are lazy."* Thus the problem might become, *"What ways might we make people less lazy?"* If the group is shown that many of the facts are thus implicitly problems, it can treat them as such and move forward. For example, taking the fact about laziness, the group can translate it into *many* Problem-Finding statements, such as, *"What ways might we get the people involved?"* *"In what ways might we get them to enjoy the work?"*

7. Sometimes people will resist lengthy Problem-Finding because they feel they already know what the problem is. In this case, try getting them to play, to experiment, to "just see what would happen if we tried for ten different definitions by viewing it in many unusual ways." Sometimes this is difficult but a breakthrough can happen if the group is encouraged to try enough alternatives.

8. If possible, the statement chosen for ideation should be one which the person has not previously explored extensively. If the problem sounds intriguing and challenging — usually because nobody before has phrased it that way or looked at that particular aspect of it — then it is likely to be a good problem for ideation.

9. In selecting the problem-statement for Idea-Finding, I usually ask if one statement jumps out as most intriguing, most potentially useful. *"If you could get some magic answers to your questions, which question would you want the magic answers to?"* This "gut level" kind of intuitive selection is often very productive. Obviously a more systematic, thorough, or logical evaluation of the different statements could be made, against criteria, exactly as is done with ideas in Solution-Finding. Sometimes this is warranted, but generally the "gut level" selection seems reasonable in a short runthrough. It frequently evolves into an adaptation of the actual original wording of the one selected — even a combining or synthesizing of it with other statements on the list.

10. It is advantageous to focus on a narrow statement of the problem — a subproblem of the general statement — as a first step. Other sub-areas can be approached later in solving the basic problem. If you try to attack the broad question and if time is limited, you may not be able to get past conventional approaches and into new areas of thinking. Hence, it is better to "divide and conquer" and work one-at-a-time with different subareas, using imagination to open up new ideas under each subproblem.

11. In Problem-Finding it is reassuring to know that research has tended to indicate the following: no matter which problem-statement is ultimately selected after a thorough search of all conceivable ways to express the problem, we will probably find that ideas generated during Idea-Finding will relate to various aspects of the problem because the many facets of it will have been brought to our conscious attention during the earlier listing of diverse IWWMI questions. Thus, even when focussing on the selected way of viewing and approaching the problem, related connections to other relevant aspects of the problem will be more likely to occur in our thinking.

12. Playing with verbs in the chosen statement can be helpful. We might ask the group to list approximate synonyms instead of the verb in the problem-statement. We often change our mental "set" by doing this. It can also be done with other key words in the problem-statement. The best choice is then used in the final wording of the problem-statement which is taken into Idea-Finding. If several words seem equally intriguing, all can be used as triggers in the problem-statement "headline" to Idea-Finding.

13. Try to word the selected problem-statement concisely. Think of it as a "telegram." This keeps it sharply in the group's focus as the statement heading the list of ideas to follow.

IDEA-FINDING:

1. To begin Idea-Finding, highlight the selected "In what ways might I?" question developed in Problem-Finding. This should begin a flow of ideas. If additional stimulation is needed, processes like the idea-spurring verbs (magnify, minify, rearrange) can be used productively, either on the question itself or on individual ideas already listed.

2. Urge people to avoid asking questions during Idea-Finding. Point out that when that happens they are really judging the appropriateness of a thought or idea. They may assume anything they want and just let ideas come. Later, during judging and selecting, the relevance can be assessed by the client or group.

3. Urge the group to avoid "editorializing" — that is, defending or elaborating on an idea to justify it. This is unnecessary during deferred judgment.

4. Urge people to give both obvious and original ideas and not to worry about repetition. It is often faster to relist ideas than to see if they are already there. Furthermore, checking for possible repetition tends to make us ask ourselves if each additional thought has already been listed, thus slowing down the process. Each is usually said somewhat differently anyhow, which may trigger other connections.

5. Urge the group to "hitch-hike" — to combine, adapt and improve ideas others suggest.

6. In Idea-Finding and in the deferred-judgment phase of any other step, it is often helpful to generate physical movement among the group — for example, by having a person run to the board and write an idea as it is spoken. Everything that can be done throughout the session to maintain physical activity as well as the mental and emotional

stimulation that takes place during a brainstorming session is helpful.

7. Relationships can be "forced" between anything in our awareness and either the problem or any idea already on the list, in order to generate new ideas.

8. Press for analogies. These can be extremely productive.

9. If the list has general ideas (approaches) some may be broken down into many specific ideas.

10. Imagery processes can be used. For example, *"Take an imaginary trip to Africa or to your favorite vacation spot. Bring back something and connect it with the situation at hand or with ideas already listed, to generate new ideas."*

11. Take some "silly" ideas on the list and turn them into good ones by adapting or modifying. That shows the value of allowing and encouraging "silly" ideas during deferred judgment.

12. Read every third, sixth or eighth idea and see what new ideas are triggered by relating them out of their original sequence.

13. Try to get people past merely purging known experiences from their minds. Encourage adaptations, combinations, or new connections where "ahas" are more likely to occur for more people. But remember, the listing of known experiences is valuable in itself, particularly if the thoughts expressed are new to others in the group. For more on this, see Chapter 15.

14. To help decide when to move from Idea-Finding to Solution-Finding, consider whether there have been some productive *"ahas."* Has the group had some exciting idea-flurries? Does the client see some intriguing ideas? If not, you probably haven't gone far enough. Try some specific techniques to break past the obvious. But, if time is short and the client seems to have some interesting possibilities, this is a good clue to begin moving to the next step.

SOLUTION-FINDING:

Note: This step is often confusing because in every other step there is a "searching" included under the step's "topic." Under Fact-Finding there is a search for facts; under Problem-Finding, a search for problems; under Idea-Finding, a search for ideas. But under Solution-Finding, the search is for "criteria," not solutions. However, in this step we are seeking tentative solutions by combining groups of ideas into possible solutions or plans in a free-wheeling synthesis process, before we apply the criteria. Thus, we might consider Solution-Finding to be a free-wheeling, deferred-judgment attempt to combine, rearrange, and adapt thoughts from the Idea-Finding stage into potential problem-solutions or plans, followed by ideation for criteria and their application to potential solutions or plans.

It is also well to emphasize that application of criteria is always implicit, even if not made explicit, at the end of every step of the process, not just in Solution-Finding. The difference is that it becomes "explicit" in Solution-Finding.

In other words, we implicitly develop criteria and apply them throughout the process. (We judge which facts are more important than others and which problems are more appropriate or important.) In Solution-Finding this notion of listing and applying criteria to the solution-possibilities is made explicit. We thus emphasize a four-step process: (1) listing potential solution-possibilities (the syntheses and recombination of the most attractive raw ideas from the Idea-Finding stage); (2) identifying criteria for evaluating these possibilities; (3) selecting the most appropriate and important criteria; (4) applying the selected criteria to the solution-possibilities to determine the best ones — or we use the chosen criteria as a checklist for improving and refining a solution we already know we would like to use. In all other steps we use the same four-step process implicitly, but in Solution-Finding we always make this implicit process explicit before moving into the final phase of Acceptance-Finding and Action — when the ideas move from thoughts into actual behavior.

1. If the group is familiar and comfortable with the word "criteria," lead into Solution-Finding by asking participants to list criteria for use in evaluating the ideas, just as you seek flow in every other step.

2. To glean new criteria about ideas being considered for evaluation, ask *"who else?"* or *"what else?"* might use, see, or care about them. Then ask what that person would look for, or even what that "thing" would look for. If we were looking for criteria to evaluate an improvement on an automobile, we might ask, *"What would the mechanic look for?" "What would the garage look for?" "What would the cat look for?" "What would the baby look for?" "What would so and so look for or want?"* This enables people to get the notion of criteria from various viewpoints in order to discover important criteria they might otherwise overlook.

3. Another technique for developing criteria is to concentrate on the advantages or disadvantages of ideas under consideration.

4. Another method is the "PMI" of well-known author Edward deBono. This stands for pluses, minuses and interesting points about the idea. These pluses, minuses and interesting points that are discovered to be inherent in a particular idea on a list can also be used as yardsticks to evaluate all of the other ideas that are being considered on the total list.

5. *"What's good about it?"* and *"What's bad about it?"* are additional stimuli to focus on ideas when searching out criteria.

6. *"Who or what might be affected?" "What are the conceivable repercussions or consequences?" "What might make the idea fail?" "What might make it succeed or improve?"* These questions lead to the realization of criteria.

7. The phrase "Will it . . . ?" or "Will the idea . . . ?" can be used effectively as a lead-in to the wording of criteria, just as IWWMI can be an effective lead-in to the Problem-Finding question. Example: *"Will the idea be cost-effective?"* This focuses on the judicial question implicit in any criterion.

8. To encourage a diverse flow of criteria, use trigger questions like:

- What things do you like about your idea or plan? What might make you like it better?
- What are interesting aspects of it?
- What are the advantages?
- What concerns you about it?
- What are the disadvantages?
- What do you wish the approach or idea or plan would do?
- What might others wish the approach or idea or plan would do?
- What *else* might you or others *like* it to do?
- What are conceivable implications, consequences of acting on the idea or plan? Short range? Long range?
- What might hinder you from doing it? Doing it well? Gracefully? Economically?

9. A kind of general evaluation checklist that might be used and expanded upon with specifics includes:

Effect on objective?
Individuals and/or groups affected?
Costs involved?
Tangibles involved (materials, equipment)?
Moral and/or legal implications?

"IT MAY VERY WELL BRING ABOUT IMMORTALITY, BUT IT WILL TAKE FOREVER TO TEST IT."

© 1996 by Sidney Harris

Intangibles involved (opinions, attitudes, feelings, aesthetic values)?

New problems caused?

Difficulties of implementation and follow-up?

Repercussions of failure?

Timeliness?

10. Criteria-listing as a means of demonstrating how easily important criteria may be overlooked can also be used. Whenever the group feels it has the pertinent criteria, I ask it to draw a line, and then go wild in search of additional criteria. I urge it to empathize with anybody or anything in the situation. *"Try to list criteria coming to mind from anybody's point of view or anything's point of view."* When group members ultimately choose the most important criteria to evaluate and develop their ideas, they invariably include some from those they listed below the line. These can become criteria which, when ignored, elicit the later reaction, "Oh, why didn't I think of that?; I could kick myself!" — when they use an idea not adequately evaluated earlier.

11. "Wants" and "musts" are other words useful in seeking additional criteria. What might I or others *want* in the ideas? What *must* the ideas do to meet my own needs and desires, as well as external constraints? Adapt the idea to make it better meet the "wants" and "musts" as we move into Acceptance-Finding.

12. In Solution-Finding we do not usually use the evaluation matrix unless the group is trying to reach a consensus on a decision. There the matrix can be extremely helpful. Or, if the individual or group is having difficulty choosing from among several desirable alternatives, the matrix can also be very helpful. But when someone has ideas or a plan he or she would like to use, but knows they would not meet certain criteria, the productive approach seems to dictate selecting these pet ideas or plans and refining them, using the criteria as focal points to improve the ideas. For example, if an idea costs too much, develop ways to reduce costs or to provide substitutes. Considering our "pet solution," choose as criteria everything that might get in the way of accomplishing it, and then brainstorm for ways to overcome these difficulties. This is actually a lead-in to Acceptance-Finding.

Try applying criteria to improve their idea or plan. The following 25 questions on improvement imply broad, general criteria, which can trigger many specific ideas when brainstorming ways of addressing each of those criteria.

Thus the "criteria listing" is used to lead into idea-production for making the idea or plan more suitable, workable, and acceptable, on each major criterion. We build "next year's improvements" into "this year's model," instead of discovering the shortcomings after the fact.

In what ways might I improve the idea or plan?
- To make it more effective?
- To increase its potential payoff?
- To make it more practical, workable?
- To make it better serve my objective?
- To make it more pleasing to me and others?
- To make it more acceptable to me and others?
- To reap more benefits from it?
- To make it less costly?
- To make it more morally or legally acceptable?
- To get more rewards and recognition from it?
- To require less resources?
- To enrich its by-products?
- To increase its appeal?
- To gain more encouragement from others?
- To mitigate problems it might cause?
- To salvage more if it should fail?
- To make it easier to implement?
- To make it easier to follow up?
- To lessen risks or results of failure?
- To give me more confidence in its working?
- To make it more timely?
- To add fringe benefits?
- To make it easier to test?
- To enable taking first steps more easily?
- To make it *better* in each respect listed in Number 8 above.

To stretch your imagination even more, try exaggerating some criteria. For example, instead of "to make it less costly," say, "to make it free," or "to make it pay me instead of costing."

One can also take the "ideal solution" desired and visualize the idea at work, if only in a fantasy way. Then work creatively to build it into practicality, adapting it to the realities of the criteria just as we practice turning "silly" ideas into good ones. Imagery processes can be very helpful here.

13. Synectics'® "itemized response" is another effective procedure. Ask the client what he or she *likes* about the idea or plan, listing several responses. Then ask what is *not liked* about it, or for concerns about it, listing whatever is stated. The group then leads into Acceptance-Finding with ways to overcome the "dislikes" or "concerns" (in other words, the criteria on which it rates poorly).

14. As pointed out under "Process Refinements Never End!" in my introductory "Reflections" on page xviii, we can bring about intuitive awareness of criteria by simply focussing on ways to *improve* selected ideas or a rough plan. By pushing for more and more improvements, we increase sensitivity to deficiencies — intuitive awareness of more and more criteria. Then, if desired, the list in Number 12 can be used to stimulate an even greater flow of improvements by breaking down the improvements into specific categories.

ACCEPTANCE-FINDING:

1. To lead into Acceptance-Finding, one of the best ways I know is to write down the idea or plan to be implemented and say, *"Let's list all the ways we can think of to get this idea or plan into operation — to gain acceptance of it."* Then simply go for a free flow of deferred-judgment thoughts about it; if you need stimulation use the "who," "what," "where," "when," "why" and "how" questions. Be careful to use them in a forward thrusting, option-seeking way. For example, Who all *might* help me? What resources *might* I use? What alternative times (when) and places (where) *might* be advantageous? How *might* I gain acceptance? What advantages *might* the ideas have to others (why)? These are analogous to the IWWMI question used as the lead-in to Idea-Finding. The thoughts in Acceptance-Finding *are* actually more ideas, but hopefully more specific, action-oriented ones than in Idea-Finding.

2. When moving to Acceptance-Finding, be careful not to converge immediately on a *specific* who, what, when, where, why or how. This is a common mistake of inexperienced facilitators. It results in a Plan of Action without providing the strength of the divergent stretch of generating many alternatives. The plan itself is the convergent stage of Acceptance-Finding. After having listed many alternatives, *then* zero in on the *best* ones for the Plan of Action.

3. Unless there is a reason for obtaining group consensus, let each individual take his or her chosen idea(s) and begin Acceptance-Finding alone or with a partner. Of course, if it is a client's problem,

Acceptance-Finding can be done by the group on the client's selection of ideas. In each case, use criteria selected from the Solution-Finding stage to trigger new thoughts for acceptance and meeting the criteria. In effect, each person is "tailoring" the idea in accordance with his or her selected criteria. Each criterion becomes a lever — a working tool — for pushing the idea into greater effectiveness. Each criterion suggests IWWMI questions. For example, if money is a critical criterion *"IWWMI reduce costs?"* or *"IWWMI get more funds?"*

4. To continue Acceptance-Finding, keep asking for ways to gain acceptance — to put the idea to use — to insure success — to improve it — to show advantages — to gain enthusiasm — to overcome objections — to anticipate misconceptions — and to pretest it. Emphasize imagery processes to stimulate flow of thoughts.

5. Try for verifiable, specific thoughts. For example, not *"cut down on smoking,* "but *"smoke one cigarette less each day until extinction."*

6. The following 30-question checklist is an extension of the Who, What, When, Where, Why and How questions. They are all worded in a positive, alternative-seeking way, implying or using the verb "might."

The 30 questions also deal with many general criteria. Hence they can be used effectively to combine Solution-Finding and Acceptance-Finding. If the questions are earnestly applied to an idea one wants to implement, the responses will provide ways for moving the idea into an effective Plan of Action — in full awareness of criteria. Choices are made of the best responses under the various questions in narrowing down to a Plan of Action.

Follow or adapt the plan below with the participants.

- **"Implementation-Expansion: 30 Questions"**[9]

  Idea or plan to be Implemented:

  (Write the idea, or problem-solution, you propose to put into effect. It should be one that is not easy to implement, and one on which you would be willing to expend a great deal of energy to accomplish.)

  Questioning Procedure:

  A. List immediate thoughts in response to each of the following questions. If a question does not trigger any response, go on to the next, completing the list as rapidly as possible.

B. After going through the full list of questions once, try for a different viewpoint by asking the reverse of each question or by giving each question an opposite twist. For example, with question No. 1: What might you *not* do to gain acceptance? This will often bring important factors into your awareness.

C. After processing the list with the opposite approach, attempt to *diverge* still more in response to each question. You may do so by having a partner press you repeatedly for multiple responses to each question, by brainstorming each question with a partner, or by other variations to introduce *stretch* — extended effort toward multiple alternatives regarding each question.

D. When you have exhausted the possibilities for responding to each question, choose the best answers in developing an actual action plan to follow in implementing your idea.

Questions:

1. What might I do to gain acceptance? How? When? Where? Why?
2. What might I do to gain enthusiasm for the idea? How? When? Where? Why?
3. What might I do to insure effectiveness? How? When? Where? Why?
4. What ways might I use criteria to show advantages? How might I demonstrate or dramatize these? Where? When? Why?
5. What other advantages might there be? How might I dramatize these? When? Where? Why?
6. What disadvantages might there be? How might I overcome these? When? Where? Why?
7. What additional resources might help (individuals, groups, money, materials, equipment, time, authority, permission, other tangibles, etc.)? How might I obtain them? When? Where? Why?
8. What new challenges might the idea suggest?

© The Creative Problem Solving Group — Buffalo, 1996.
Used with permission.

9. How might I anticipate and meet these? When? Where? Why?

10. What objections, difficulties, limitations, obstacles might there be?

11. How might I overcome them? When? Where? Why?

12. How might I improve, safeguard, or fortify the idea? When? Where? Why?

13. Who might help with the idea? How? When? Where? Why?

14. What groups might help? How? When? Where? Why?

15. Who might contribute special strengths or resources? How? When? Where? Why? How might I get them to help? When? Where? Why?

16. Who might add an unexpected element? How? When? Where? Why?

17. Who might gain from the idea? What might I do to make it easier to understand and appreciate? How? When? Where? Why?

18. Who might need persuasion? In what ways might I make it simpler, less complex for them? How? When? Where? Why?

19. How might I reward myself or others for helping carry out the idea? When? Where? Why?

20. How might I pretest my idea? When? Where? Why?

21. What first steps might I take to initiate action? To get into action faster? How? When? Where? Why?

22. What next steps might follow? How? When? Where? Why?

23. What timing might I use? How? When? Where? Why?

24. What schedules might I follow? How? When? Where? Why?

25. What follow-up might provide feedback to measure the progress? How? When? Where? Why?

26. What follow-up might allow corrective measures? How? When? Where? Why?

27. What follow-up might deal with unexpected repercussions? How? When? Where? Why?

28. What special times might I use? Days? Dates? How? Where? When? Why?
29. What special circumstances or occasions might I use? How? When? Where? Why?
30. What special places or locations might I use? How? When? Where? Why?

7. Try using the morphological approach. List many "who's," "what's," "where's," "when's," "how's," "why's," and then cross-relate the items randomly under the various headings, for a variety of potential plans. Some will be obvious, while most will probably take considerable creative development to make them workable. I often have participants put adverbs under the "how" column to see what thoughts they suggest. For example, slowly, cautiously, recklessly, joyously. Under "why," I have them put aspects of criteria, such as *to keep costs down,* *to make the boss happy.*

8. In deciding when to close in on the Plan of Action, watch for real "hits" or "ahas" in Acceptance-Finding. The more stretch, the more likelihood some of these "ahas" will be experienced. If that happens, the plan will be richer, more interesting and more motivating.

9. In Acceptance-Finding as in Solution-Finding, it is usually advisable to have individuals make convergent judgments alone or in teams of two, rather than try to do this in subgroups or in the entire group. It is important to do it in the total group or in sub-groups only when the Plan of Action is of importance to all involved. In that case one needs consensus and the time it takes to develop that is worth spending. On the other hand, if an *individual* decision and Plan of Action is all that is needed, there is no use taking the time and energy to get group consensus unless the client desires it.

PLAN OF ACTION:

1. If time permits, have the client go back through all the subproblems and ideas to glean anything that might be usable in the Plan of Action.

2. Be sure the client gives a first step to be taken within the next few days or week at most. It might be merely a phone call or memo, but it should be something to get the idea moving. Be sure the client describes, as part of the plan, just when he or she will go back to earlier subproblems or ideas in attempting to resolve the entire

problem — of which the first specific idea implemented may only be a small part.

3. One last step I often take is to have the person think of the analogy of a gourmet meal in relation to the Plan of Action. *"List what the 'appetizer' might be that could be added to the plan to make it richer."* Next, *"What 'spices or dressing' might be added if your plan were a meal?"* Lastly, *"If your plan were a meal, what might be the 'dessert'?"* This will often trigger additions or improvements worthwhile to the client. Of course other analogies could be equally productive.

4. Emphasize that "nothing is final," but that it is the best plan presently available. Urge the client to remain open to other thoughts as long as possible without unduly delaying action, and to incorporate improvements where possible before taking action.

5. Point out that it is unnecessary to have an "aha" to have accomplishment. The chosen plan may be prosaic, but dormant before being awakened by the process. Very likely some "ahas" have occurred, including some "negative ahas" perhaps — ones which warn of pitfalls in various ideas which might have been applied. Sometimes the most obvious idea may be the best and the balance of the process provides motivation to implement an idea that had been dormant all the time.

6. I frequently conclude by having individuals image their plans of action *in effect* — then add any modifications seen or felt during the imaging. This can also serve to help them make commitments to their plans — particularly if I urge them during the imaging to feel the pride of accomplishment, the satisfaction of achievement, etc.

Conclusion

In all the thoughts expressed in each of the divergent steps, one might assess the effectiveness of the divergence by measuring the fluency, flexibility, and originality under each step. The Plan of Action can be assessed by the elaboration, the sensitivity to new challenges or problems, and ultimately by its impact potential; how well does it meet the objective or deal with the mess? Thus we see evidence throughout the process of five major creativity-measurement factors: fluency, flexibility, originality, elaboration, and sensitivity to problems, plus the "ultimate criterion" of impact on the objective or mess.

CHAPTER FIFTEEN

Three Levels Of Brainstorming: Toward A New Appreciation Of "ING"

The skilled facilitator probably recognizes at least three levels of brainstorming for ideas. The first is when we share facts rather than ideas. That is, I get the freedom not to be judged, criticized, or analyzed for what I say; therefore I feel free to say whatever I know and not worry about the value judgments of others. So, I share things that I've done before that might be appropriate to the moment. I pull these out of my experience and share them. And if they are new to the other person, then the other person may have an "aha." At any rate, the person suggesting the idea is *not* having an "aha," but is releasing a bit of data already held. It's a valuable type of session, and many sessions are of this type, particularly with inexperienced brainstormers.

The second level of brainstorming involves the situation where I want to become original in my approach or else I've run out of things to say. As advertising executive Willard Pleuthner (BBD&O) once put it, *"I've cleared the cobwebs out of my brain."* In the latter case, I have nowhere to go to produce more ideas other than to deliberately combine, rearrange, or adapt ideas of my own or of other members of the group in *new* ways. These ideas become the combination or adaptation of known elements. That *new* configuration becomes the idea and the newness in the configuration provides the "aha" to the person generating the idea, and perhaps to others if it's new to them as well. In this second level of brainstorming, there is more excitement and more "ahas" take place.

The third level of brainstorming is similar to what the writer or artist experiences when the "article takes over" or the "painting takes over." Famous artists, writers, and other creative people have often referred to this phenomenon, where the material flows from their minds without deliberate effort. It's as though the spontaneous "right-brain" has taken over. It's almost orgasmic. When this happens in a brainstorming session, the ideas flow for at least some of the participants without

FRANK & ERNEST reprinted by permission of
Newspaper Enterprise Association, Inc.

FRANK & ERNEST® by Bob Thaves

trying to make it happen; it just takes place and is exciting and exhilarating. This does not happen frequently. In my own experience it is relatively rare to have any length of that type of session.

Recently I had such an experience where the "ahas" were almost continuous, and of different levels of voltage, as I put it, from 1 volt to 110 volts, with almost a constant surge of current going through the group — or at least through my mind — as I was participating in this brainstorming session. It had very deep meaning to me because, for the past 40 years, I've been in conference after conference where I have attempted, with others, to define creativity — to understand it more deeply. This session provided insights and depth of understanding I had never known before.

We developed the concept of "ing" having a new meaning well beyond my understanding of what the suffix ever meant.* Let's take a couple of examples. Compare "think" with "thinking." If I say, "He *thinks,* as in *"He thinks she is an unpleasant person,"* "think" connotes that "he is of the opinion" or "he has formed the closure" or "he has formed the stance, the closed convergent stance," that this is so. But, if I say, *"He is thinking about her personality,"* this could connote an examination of all aspects of her personality and an attempt to understand the fullness of this unique being, whom he will never fully comprehend. Maybe another way to say it would be to use Maslow's concept of "self-actualize." If I say, *"I am self-actualized,"* I am being closed; I am *there;* I have arrived and there is nowhere farther to go. If I say I am a self-actualiz*ing* individual, it means that I am on a quest for infinite fulfillment, which is never attainable but is a constant quest. And for that self-actualiz*ing,* the "ing" is that quest; it is that infinite, divergent openness toward something that never arrives — never closes — never is final.

Take the word "notice." I say, *"I notice this."* It tells me that I see this; I observe this particular detail as a finite closed observation. If I say, *"I am noticing some things about you, about this,"* it may imply that I am carefully observing and that I am taking in more and more; I am beginning to get a greater clarity about the meaning of you, or it, but I will *never* have the total meaning of you or anything. Notic*ing* has a tentative, open stance that notice does not imply. It is a fine difference and maybe I am splitting hairs, but to me it is exciting

*I wish to acknowledge Robert Johnston for stimulating my thinking about the levels of brainstorming, and the members of the group, at the "Second Whole-Brained Symposium" in Key West, Florida, who triggered my "third level" experience with "ing": Carol Berns, Ned Herrmann, Barbara Robey, Dick Thorn and Helena Toner.

and really gets at the essence of creativity because when one is being creative, one is be*ing*. One is not *be;* one is not *is;* one is be*ing,* becom*ing.* The "ing" is the essence of creativity. The "ing" connotes that constant divergent searching, option-seeking — what "deferred judgment" in Osborn's terms was all about — what "spontaneity" in Moreno's terms was all about — what any system of exploring in Synectics, or Prince's "experimental self," was all about — or what Barron's "tolerance of ambiguity" was all about. It's that openness, tentativeness, lack of closure.

I once coined the term "deferjudiced." Now I like "deferjudicing" better! It means that I am deferring judgment and taking in ever more factors between stances of closure — when I *must* close. I must make decisions, but if I am "deferjudicing" I am being more and more open to greater quantities of input from which to arrive at my decision. That way I am more apt to get closer to the total gestalt of something than if I have a myopic view of only part of it.

As I think and write about the "ing" notion, I am becoming aware of more aspects of it. Notice the five steps in our creative problem-solving model are "Fact-Find*ing,* Problem-Find*ing,* Idea-Find*ing,* Solution-Find*ing,* and Acceptance-Find*ing.*" I don't remember that wording being deliberate; we might have used the words "Fact-Find, Problem-Find, etc.," without having realized the difference. But today, the difference is powerful to me. It connotes that we never find all the facts or the problem definitions. Perhaps we intuitively chose adding the "ing" to the steps without realizing its power and relevance. Or perhaps Osborn understood this difference very well and deliberately used "ing" as he did in his early emphasis, calling for Fact-Find*ing,* Idea-Find*ing,* and Solution-Find*ing.*

George Land and Vaune Ainsworth applied "ing" to truth and came up with truth*ing.* I like that concept which means that truth is never final. It is only a goal. They summarized:

The process of "ing" keeps us alive and moves us along the evolutionary scale toward the process of god-ing.

I have enjoyed applying the "ing" to many words and find it fascinating. I hope others will do likewise. Even my favorite "aha" becomes less final, more tentative and open to refinement and new meanings, when we speak of "aha-*ing.*"

The "ing" notion is evident in the summary I have prepared about the philosophy and stages of the creative problem-solving process in the following chapter.

CHAPTER SIXTEEN

How Might We Summarize
A CPS Experiential Workshop?

NOTE: Although I prepared the following as a summary and conclusion, participants reading it suggested strongly that it would have been helpful at the very beginning, as an introduction. So I now provide it right at the start of a workshop. Both participants and facilitators find it useful then as well as for review at the conclusion of the program.

If you know more about CPS than you did when you started, but are understanding that there's a lifetime of learning about internalizing it for ever-greater effectiveness, then you may be truly "knowing" CPS in the sense of the previous chapter. If you are gaining a more creative attitude, you probably are "knowing" CPS better than you would by gaining the fullest intellectual understanding of the specifics of the CPS model. This more creative attitude can become a way of life rather than a set of procedures. With it you can keep inventing your own CPS model and techniques; the model you practiced serves mainly for developing that creative attitude which I hope you continue to nourish.

What do I mean by this creative attitude? Here is my summary:

- In Objective-Finding (What I call "the front end of the process"):

    A "pro-acting" stance; looking for more and more opportunities in all aspects of life — not merely "re-acting" to what happens — and choosing the most promising prospects to process.

    FOCUS: *Wishing, dreaming, imagining, fantasying, challenging* — to discover more and more objectives and opportunities for CPS.

- In Fact-Finding:

Searching for ever-more details, relationships, implications in everything in our awareness; using all our senses and feelings to examine everything ever-more deeply before making judgments.

> FOCUS: Who, What, Where, When, Why, How *(Is and Is Not).*

- In Problem-Finding:

Seeking more and more new ways to view people, situations, and things — to view and express problems, challenges, and opportunities — from diverse perspectives — and choosing the best ones for creative response.

> FOCUS: "In What Ways Might I . . . ?"

- In Idea-Finding:

Seeking more and more diverse ideas, alternatives, options, paths, means, or approaches through a variety of methods and techniques — and then choosing the most promising ones for detailed evaluating and developing.

> FOCUS: Making new relationships, associations, connections. MAGNIFYING, MINIFYING, REARRANGING.

- In Solution-Finding:

Examining ideas or plans in more and more diverse ways, from ever-more viewpoints and criteria; becoming aware of more and more consequences, implications, repercussions of a tentative idea or solution; seeking *improvements.*

> FOCUS: Effect on whom? Effect on what? Will the idea . . . ? MUSTS and WANTS.

- In Acceptance-Finding:

  Seeking ever-more ways of making idea-solutions more workable, more acceptable, stronger, or more effective.

  > FOCUS: In What Ways Might I get this idea moving? Who might? What might? When might? Where might? Why might? How might? Who else? What else? Etc.? — And how about might *not?*

- In Taking Action:

  Making more and more happen — making ever-more small starts. Planning for more and more next steps. Turning ever-more *wishes* into *actions* — taking one *constructive action* rather than making 100 New Year's resolutions that are only *intentions.*

  > FOCUS: Recognizing that "nothing is final" — nothing is "black or white"; today's best plan becoming tomorrow's challenge for improvement. "Everything becoming relative."

- In General:

  "Deferjudicing" — flowing ever-more freely in any "step" of the process before judging; taking more and more factors into consideration, in a *given* unit of time, in making a decision or taking action; then recognizing the decision or action as only the best one for the moment, but that:

  > A fair idea put to use is better than a good idea kept on the polishing wheel.

  > — Alex F. Osborn

I live my life by Osborn's credo and with the creative attitude I've stressed. Over the years I have been heartened to see the rapidly growing numbers of individuals, groups, and organizations that are acquiring these attitudes and behaving accordingly in their lives. The ultimate will be when all nations do the same.

Conclusion

In pursuing our desires, we proceed from examining "what *is*" to exploring "what *might* be," to judging "what *ought* to be," to assessing "what *can presently* be," to deciding "what *I will commit to do now*," to action that becomes a new "what *is.*"

- "What is" refers to your awareness of the facts or data about a situation.

- "What might be" implies the generation of multiple-viewpoint, forward-thrusting definitions, approaches, and ideas toward the realization of objectives.

- "What ought to be" involves considered judgments about approaches and ideas.

- "What can presently be" refers to your choices and adaptations of approaches and ideas into what seems to be a manageable solution for now.

- "What I will commit to do now" becomes your best plan for gaining acceptance and implementing.

- "Action" becomes your actual *doing, implementing,* including checking results and making adjustments — all of which brings about the new "is."

Out of subsequent deeper examination of our action and its results — the new "what is" — grow new challenges and problems to be handled through the CPS process, culminating in further action which again becomes another *new* "what is," and so on!

Let me now relate the above to the steps in the CPS process. Using this process, instead of merely reacting in a habitual way to what you see, in reality or in your visions and dreams, you (1) re-examine for more facts — "Fact-Finding," (2) redefine the situation from its first appearance — "Problem-Finding," (3) generate alternative ideas as reactions or responses to the situation as now viewed — "Idea-Finding," (4) evaluate and improve against multiple repercussions and con-sequences — "Solution-Finding," and (5) develop the best ideas as fully as manageable before putting them to use — "Acceptance-Finding."

The end point thus involves *acting* on *good* ideas — ones which bring positive results to the person, the organization, the society. In so doing, we follow up by monitoring for and handling new challenges growing out of the changes introduced by our actions.

Reprinted with permission of Eastman Chemical Company.

©1971 King Features Syndicate.
Reprinted with special permission of King Features Syndicate.

Epilogue

Imagination is more important than knowledge. — **Albert Einstein**

More changes in the way we live on our planet and within the universe itself, have occurred during the past hundred years than had occurred cumulatively in previous human history. And, changes beyond our wildest dreams will continue to occur even more rapidly over the next one hundred years.

Our ability to adapt to such changes, while continuing to live without destroying ourselves or our planet, lies within our ability to think creatively. Without it, these massive, rapid changes in the norms of life would drive most of us mad or to extinction like the dinosaurs. As it is, cultures worldwide are exhibiting extreme symptoms, diseases of stress, and other extraordinary diseases because new ways of thinking are replacing comfortable old mind sets too fast for comfortable adaptation.

One of the many paradoxes of life is that human nature has a dual nature regarding change. While one component seeks and welcomes change, an equally strong component resists it and in an often self-destructive, perverse manner may persecute the very people who can instruct us on how to deal creatively with change. Heroes — the likes of Socrates, Columbus, Galileo, Jesus, Darwin, Madame Curie, and King — live on the cutting edge of change and possess the courage and self-reliance to envision and promote new paradigms in the face of severe criticism, mockery, or persecution.

In these times of massive change, the creative individual and the creative society will fare best; or in the worst scenario, be the most likely to survive. They will employ holistic thinking whereby divergent, intuitive, creative thinking will work in harmony and mutuality with the analytical, convergent, "one plus one equals two" thinking currently favored.

American education, which emphasizes, teaches, and rewards students who demonstrate high language and mathematical skills, must

By Robert A. Partridge, M.D.

expand its scope to include a balanced teaching and reward system for such equally and essential human skills as creativity, the arts, interpersonal skills, intrapersonal skills, and kinesthetics. Examples of the effective use of holistic thinking can be found in the industrial, educational, and governmental systems of countries which are most successful in dealing with rapid change. In Japan, Germany, Korea, and Taiwan, themes of cooperation, mutuality, and synergy between government, business, and education are the norm, replacing adversarial or mutually exclusive relationships. Concepts of continuous quality improvement foster the understanding that each individual within a society has extremely creative and useful thoughts and ideas to contribute — through team effort — to viable change and significant improvement in the ways things are done.

In this respect, it is critical to understand that every human being possesses significant creative abilities. However, emphasis on IQ tests and didactic analytical thinking has frequently hampered the recognition and nurturance of the 120 different, special, and measurable aspects of creative thinking which particularly distinguish humans from other species. These wide-ranging creative faculties have been, and continue to be, critical to mankind's ability to adapt to changing situations, environments, and systems.

Unfortunately, Sigmund Freud's erroneous linking of artistry and creativity with mental illness was subscribed to by many Western cultures, particularly our own. Consequently, this adaptation stigmatized creative thinking for too many of us. It artificially separated and compartmentalized our innate creative thinking from our other innate and intellectual abilities.

Extensive studies of creative thinking have firmly established that individuals exhibiting higher than average scores in creative thinking also exhibit higher than average scores in areas of mental/emotional health. Dr. Calvin Taylor, while professor at the University of Utah, reported evidence also suggesting creative individuals are more devoted to autonomy, more self-sufficient, more independent in judgment, more open to the irrational in themselves, more stable, more capable of taking greater risks in hopes of greater gain, more dominant and self-assertive, more self-accepting, more resourceful and adventurous, more controlling of their own behavior by self concept, and more complex as a person. Systematic courses of instruction in applied imagination produce significant gains in personality traits such as confidence, self reliance, persuasiveness, initiative, and leadership potential.

Recognition of the varied creative skills innate in each of us must become the new, major emphasis at all levels of education, beginning at the earliest stages and continuing throughout one's life. This must be followed by fostering and teaching both the understanding and the ability to utilize these varied skills fully and in concert with our other intellectual abilities. The ability to achieve effective balance between divergent, imaginative, creative thinking and convergent, "fact-oriented" thinking must become a part of every individual's education experience.

By employing concepts of teamwork, so effectively utilized in many venues of our lives, we can maximize the potential of the special and different kinds of creative skills found in varied and different individuals, nations, or cultures. As a football team uses a coach, quarterback, fullback, tight end, center, tackle, punter, various defensive specialists and special team players, teams composed of creative thinkers trained and coached to utilize each member's particularly strong creative skills will become the norm. These teams will deal more effectively with a multitude of wide-ranging concerns such as world peace, quality of life, product quality improvements, win-win relationships of individuals and nations, and effective contact with other life forms in the universe.

In November, 1989, the years 1990-1999 were aptly designated as the Decade of the Brain by a Joint Congressional Resolution signed by President George Bush. New scientific techniques such as computerized tomography (CT), brain electrical activity mapping (BEAM), magnetic resonance imaging (MRI), single-proton emission computed tomography (SPECT), and positron emission tomography (PET) are at this very moment more clearly defining the structure and dynamic function of the brain and determining what areas of the brain are operant during specific thinking processes. Current studies by the National Institutes of Health into meditation, acupuncture, and other alternative medical treatments will more clearly define how and why these time-tested methods work within the brain and the brain/mind/body connection.

Another emerging feature of the adult brain is revolutionizing the way scientists now think about both brain injury and everyday cognition. It was previously believed that the brain was highly dynamic only in infancy and childhood, especially during crucial periods of development. It had been felt that after a certain age, brain cells knew what they were supposed to do and they did it the rest of their lives. Brain architecture was thought to be fixed, especially in the areas receiving raw information from the eyes, ears, and skin. Hence, the old adage "you can't teach an old dog new tricks." Well, as many of us already know, we can!

We know, for example, that visually, images are processed by at least thirty layers of visual cortex, each with its own architecture and rules. The largely unexplored auditory cortex is now believed to contain at least four maps specializing in different frequency ranges. Current experiments give us clues that these maps are not static and that the remapping process is both dynamic and rapid. It may be, for example, that sensory remapping occurs in fractions of milliseconds. This probably applies to many other (or perhaps all) levels of the brain and brain function, as well.

Until recently, scientists believed that nerve cells in the brain died if the body part to which they were connected was lost. Now, however, it appears that the brain does not have fixed circuits. Rather, in ways that are still unknown, the adult brain appears to be capable of reorganizing and rewiring itself over incredibly large distances. This can be used to explain how many victims of stroke or other neurological injury have made dramatic recoveries. Examples of brain "rewiring" or "remapping" are also seen everyday in psychotherapy. Old "tapes", "circuits", or "maps" relating to self-concept, relationship of self to others and/or one's environment, and ultimately the way we think are constantly extruded, modified, or "rewired" — sometimes slowly and sometimes rapidly — resulting in healthier, richer, more vital living and well-being.

When these studies and new techniques are applied to the processes of thinking, learning, memory, and creativity, the results should shake the very foundations of learning and education. Indeed, dynamic and ever-changing cortical maps may lie at the very basis of learning, memory, and creativity. The same processes may also lie in many other higher brain areas, so that who we are and what we know is constantly being reshaped by experience.

Recent studies reported at the 1992 meetings of the Society for Neuroscience concurred that the adult human brain is more dynamic than static — that it continually shapes and reshapes itself from experiences throughout life. Dr. Michael Merzenich, a neuroscientist at the University of California at San Francisco, believes that most things we don't understand about the brain will probably be explained in terms of these dynamics. Ultimately, the new models of sensory processing developed from current experiments will most probably help us understand the dynamic properties of the brain.

This will lead us to understanding and ameliorating disabilities of learning, emotional/mental/physical illnesses, and problems of the aging brain. It should, therefore, become possible to help people recover from many currently "irreversible" nervous system disorders and lead to far-reaching changes in the treatment of conditions like depression, anxiety, stroke, paralysis, spinal cord injury, other types of brain and nerve trauma, and other forms of mental/emotional/physical illness. The artificial and extremely limiting dichotomy between physical and emotional/mental illnesses and functioning will be removed as the complex interrelationship between the physical brain, thinking, intellect, creativity, intuition, and emotion is treated as a whole.

Dr. Vernon Mountcastle, neuroscientist at Johns Hopkins University, also believes that this new understanding of the dynamic brain will lead us to dramatic and fundamental new insights into learning and memory. Thus, through new understanding of the dynamic brain, we will learn the crucial coordinates of the mind which will allow us to maneuver our own intellectual rocket towards the discovery of the full potential of this amazing organ. We will become increasingly more adept both at training our brains and at maintaining levels of functioning, learning, and creativity — beyond our wildest dreams and throughout our entire lives! We will learn how to significantly accentuate certain circuits or maps and de-emphasize others, and in the process drastically and dramatically recreate, advance, and transform our entire system of education and learning. Training brains of any age to be optimally creative will ultimately enhance every aspect of our life on the planet and within the universe.

And this is only the beginning of the knowledge explosion about the brain and how we think, learn, and, yes, even how we exist! Enhanced communication and study will integrate the best of what each culture, system, and tradition has to offer in terms of maximal functioning of the mind, body, and spirit. Research and exponentially expanding knowledge of brain function will make the exploration of the brain's inner space an achievement greater than the exploration of outer space. It is now understood the brain acts in a way like a giant mainframe computer which communicates with every one of the approximately sixty trillion cells of the body. Moreover, each cell also functions like a minicomputer, with the brain and each cell, organ, and system rapidly and constantly communicating via a wide-ranging and complex network of neurotransmitters, hormones, electrical impulses, chemicals, and other forms of yet unknown communication. This network of communication facilitates the most effective interactions both within the body and in its environment — immediate, earthly, and universal. Further understanding of the brain and its creative function offer us greater hope that we may be able to more fully understand ourselves as human beings.

As one examines the spiritual literature, verifiable psychic phenomena note the brain's (mind's or spirit's) ability to communicate with other humans, if not animals, minerals, and ultimately the stars. The philosopher-poet's notion that not a leaf falls that is not felt on the furthermost star is becoming a reality. The big bang theory of the creation of the universe, quantum physics, and numerous religious/ spiritual systems consider, each in their own way, that all energy, all knowledge, all elements of the universe once existed in a microscopic seed or power which exploded or expanded to become the universe.

Extrasensory perception studies between an ESP-trained astronaut on the moon and a similarly trained astronaut on earth illustrated a significantly greater than chance ability of the moon astronaut to note which card was held by the astronaut on earth. Creative thinking allies itself with and utilizes the intuitive/psychic nature and abilities of man.

Many scholars also feel that all history, all future is held within the vast pool of the universal unconscious which is available for access to every human. An example would be the universal unconscious system described by Carl Jung. Religions or spiritual programs access this system through the powers of prayer and meditation. In a recent rigorously controlled, randomized, prospective, double blind scientific study, a computer assigned 393 patients admitted to the coronary care unit at San Francisco General Hospital either to a group that was prayed for by home prayer groups (192 patients) or to a group that was not remembered in prayer (210 patients).

It must be emphasized that the study was designed according to the most rigid criteria that can be used in clinical studies in medicine! It showed the following striking results. The prayed-for patients 1) were five times less likely than the unremembered group to require antibiotics, 2) were three times less likely to develop pulmonary edema, a condition in which the lungs fill with fluid as a consequence of the failure of the heart to pump properly, 3) required no endotracheal intubation while 12 non-prayed for patients required it, 4) resulted in fewer deaths.

Prayer was an integral part of my wife's recovery from "incurable" cancer. In 1988, after colon cancer had spread to the liver four times, and after two years of chemotherapy and seven operations had failed to stop the cancer, she was pronounced incurable. However, the power of positive thinking and prayer by thousands of caring people of many different religious or spiritual belief systems, together with a program of healthy wellness living, turned the tide. For more than six years there has been absolutely no sign of the cancer. All studies continue to be normal including a highly specific blood test (CEA) utilized monthly to detect minute amounts of cancer cells anywhere in the body. Throughout the history of mankind, many other miracles have been determined to be the result of prayer. Prayer involves another potent creative power of the mind that cannot be measured by IQ tests or by one-plus-one-equals-two thinking.

John F. Kennedy once observed that as Americans we had become accustomed to a history of rapid problem solving and resolution. He felt, however, that the major problems of our day were no longer amenable to quick solution and resolution. Instead, as in the treatment of chronic disease, he believed that these problems would not be cured but rather would be lived with and managed. This would require a new sort of effort, courage, and commitment, featuring the emotional and cognitive pacing of the marathon runner as contrasted with the hundred yard dash competitor or even the miler. Taking this a step further, I believe we now need the particular pacing of all of the different types of "runners" — be it running, walking, relying on a cane or wheelchair, or pushing a stroller — with each and every one of us utilizing our unique creative abilities to the fullest.

The communication, knowledge, and information explosion augers well for planet earth. The communication systems of the body share, coordinate, and promote the welfare of the individual, cell by cell. Improved, rapid, and effective communication of information between each individual, community, and nation — the cells of mankind — will harmonize these cells into a healthy, vital, mutually advantageous unity. The creative forces of each individual, community, and nation will be a necessary and integral part of this process. The organism of mankind will function as a whole and thereby promote maximum growth, potential, peace, and prosperity.

Footnotes

1. Page xxi.
   Finke, R. **Creative Imagery: Discoveries And Inventions In Visualization.** Hillsdale, NJ: Erlbaum Associates, 1990.

2. Page 3.
   See the following three references:
   Firestien, R. L. & McGowan, R. J. "Creative Problem-Solving And Communication Behavior In Small Groups". *Creativity Research Journal,* 1988, 1 (1).

   Murdock, M. C. & Ganim, R. M. "Creativity And Humor: Integration And Incongruity". *Journal Of Creative Behavior,* 1993, 27 (1).

   Ziv, A. **The Influence Of Humorous Atmosphere On Creativity.** Unpublished manuscript, Tel Aviv University, 1980.

3. Page 6.
   Parnes, S. J. & Noller, R. B. "Applied Creativity: The Creative Studies Project — Part II — Results Of The Two-Year Program". *Journal Of Creative Behavior,* 1972, 6 (3).

4. Page 8.
   Simberg, A. L. & Shannon, T. E. **The Effect Of AC Creativity Training On The AC Suggestion Program.** AC Spark Plug Division, General Motors Corporation (mimeo report, May 27, 1959).

5. Page 12.
   Toffler, A. **Future Shock.** NY: Random House, Inc., 1970.

6. Page 15.
   Scribner, C. Jr. **In The Company Of Writers: A Life In Publishing.** NY: Charles Scribner's Sons, 1990.

7. Page 44.
Freud, S. **The Basic Writings Of Sigmund Freud**, A. A. Brill (Ed.). NY: Random House, 1938.

8. Page 63.
Excerpts from *Western New York,* September 1992, pp. 12-13. Reprinted with permission. For additional information see: Sellick, J. A., Jr., Hazamy, P.A., and Mylotte, J. M. "Influence Of An Educational Program And Mechanical Opening Needle Disposal Boxes On Occupational Needle Stick Injuries." *Infection Control And Hospital Epidemiology,* 1991, *12,* pp. 725-731.

9. Page 139.
Noller, R. B., Parnes, S. J. & Biondi, A. M. "Implementation Expansion: 30 Questions". In Parnes, S. J. (Ed.) **Source Book For Creative Problem-Solving: A Fifty Year Digest Of Proven Innovation Processes.** Buffalo, NY: Creative Education Foundation Press, 1992.

Annotated References

The following are annotations of the fundamental works on which this present publication is based: (1) the classic books of Alex F. Osborn which provided strong roots to present-day creativity development programs and efforts; and (2) the most significant (for readers of this book) of my own writings, including one dealing with our decades of research on Creative Problem Solving (CPS).

I began my research and development work in this field of deliberate creativity-development when there was little activity or literature on the subject. Today, there is a proliferation of both. Most emanate from (1) the Osborn/Parnes principles, processes and procedures as presented in our writings and in our educational programs and (2) from Synectics®, which has also been thoroughly researched and developed in this field since the 1940's. (See Part III of **Source Book For Creative Problem-Solving** referenced below.)

Over the decades, much has been integrated within each program from the other (CPS and Synectics®). I personally have continually studied and synthesized important elements of Synectics® into the Osborn/Parnes CPS model. I have also done the same with many other emerging processes and procedures, synthesizing key aspects within our very eclectic CPS program as presented in this book.

Unfortunately, a large proportion of the literature is quite repetitive. Thus it is difficult for the serious reader to wade through the thousands of books, articles and programs to select those to study next. In 1992, I published a "mini-encyclopedia" to serve as a guide. I selected 55 key selections for publication in the **Source Book For Creative Problem-Solving: A Fifty Year Digest Of Proven Innovation Processes.**

I hope that this introduction to the references and the annotations will help you in your quest for further knowledge and growth along the infinite creativity continuum.

OSBORN:

1. Osborn, A. F. **Applied Imagination.** Buffalo, NY: Creative Education Foundation Press, 1963 (Reprinted).

   This book is a reprint of the third revised edition of Osborn's classic text in Creative Problem Solving. The author stresses the importance of imagination in all areas of life. Some of the many topics covered are: creative and non-creative forms of imagination, factors which can tend to cramp creativity, ways by which creativity can be developed, the Creative Problem-Solving process, individual ideation and team collaboration, and evolution and obsolescence of new ideas. The book is organized as a textbook, with discussion topics and exercises, as well as extensive references at the end of each chapter. It's translation into many languages, over the years, has enabled readers throughout the world to become exposed to Osborn's teachings.

2. Osborn, A. F. **Wake Up Your Mind.** NY: Scribner's, 1952 (Out-of-print).

   A book written to help readers acquire: (a) a keener REALIZATION of the fact that every individual possesses potential; (b) a stronger DESIRE to become more creative; and (c) a better UNDERSTANDING of the creative principles and procedures proven to be conducive to the improvement of creative ability. The author stresses the development of creativity throughout life — in leisure-time activities, in work, and at home.

3. Osborn, A. F. **Your Creative Power.** NY: Scribner's, 1948 (Out-of-print). A condensed version edited by Robert W. Galvin, Motorola University, is available from The Creative Education Foundation, Inc.

   Personally abridged by Robert W. Galvin, Chairman, Executive Committee, Motorola Inc., **Your Creative Power** is timeless and timely as a leadership skill tool. This shortened version is pure Osborn text retaining all of his fascinating insights and principles for stimulating individual creative power.

4. Osborn, A. F. **How To Think Up.** NY: McGraw-Hill, 1942 (Out -of-print, but the full text of this small book appears as Selection 1 of the **Source Book For Creative Problem-Solving** listed below).

This unassuming mini-book, measuring only 5 x 7 inches and 38 pages in length, was the seed from which most of today's applications of creative thinking and problem solving germinated. Osborn's prime purpose was to draw out more ideas from the 500 people in his advertising firm. Prosper Vanosmael, Professor Emeritus of English at University of Antwerp, Belgium, credited the author with breaking the 2,000 year-old paradigm that creativity could not be deliberately developed.

Many minds are of the opinion that Osborn has been responsible for bringing this paradigm shift to the consciousness of more people around the world than any other person in history.

PARNES:

1. Parnes, S. J. **Source Book For Creative Problem-Solving: A Fifty Year Digest Of Proven Innovation Processes.** Buffalo, NY: Creative Education Foundation Press, 1992.

This book provides the most comprehensive collection of valuable information available on creative problem solving – sectioned, head-noted and indexed for ease of reference. Besides introductory historical perspectives as well as theoretical roots and research foundations, it contains detailed information on: (a) CPS, Synectics® and other major ongoing programs for creativity development — their methods, tools and techniques; (b) three major current thrusts in program development: Heightened Problem-Finding, Applying Imagery/Intuition and Using Computers; (c) significant sources useful in strengthening creativity-development programs; and (d) helpful information for facilitating and instructing CPS.

The volume serves all who want an expanded understanding and appreciation of their own creative processes and how to nurture these in themselves and others — in teaching, managing, facilitating, parenting or mentoring — along an infinite continuum of possible growth in creative ability. Those who have begun developmental programs to move upward from their own particular level on that continuum will find the book invaluable toward their continuing growth — their lifetime of self-actualizing, in Maslow's terms.

The **Source Book For Creative Problem-Solving** is a "mini-encyclopedia" for trainers, teachers, practitioners, managers, parents, scholars, students and their libraries. It contains the most diverse and representative selection of relevant articles available from half a century of effort in creativity development.

2. Parnes, S. J. **Visionizing.** Buffalo, NY: Creative Education Foundation Press, 1988.

This book blends expanded imagery and analogy processes with the Osborn/Parnes Creative Problem-Solving (CPS) process. **Visionizing** serves the same purpose for the study of futuristics CPS as did the earlier Scribner publications, **Creative Behavior Guidebook, Guide To Creative Action** and **Creative Actionbook** for the general CPS programs. However, it also features and integrates researched and time-tested instructional materials from the earlier publications. The inclusion of these materials provides for three important applications: (a) to supplement, expand and make more universally applicable the sessions in Part I; (b) to help new CPS students make more powerful use of the visioning processes in Part I; and (c) to serve as general resource materials in all other types of creativity-development programs, including self-study. **Visionizing** makes explicit and expands "opportunity-finding" processes which are largely implicit in general CPS programs — in what is termed in the Osborn/Parnes model, "sensitivity to objectives or messes." It greatly expands upon "the front end of the CPS process" — the opportunity-making, the dreaming, the visioning. The dreams or visions are engineered into the best reality manageable.

3. Parnes, S. J. "The Creative Studies Project". In Isaksen, S. G. (Ed.) **Frontiers Of Creativity Research: Beyond The Basics.** Buffalo, NY: Bearly Limited, 1987.

This lengthy article capsulizes my 30 years of continuing research into the deliberate development of creative ability. Large portions of material are drawn from a major report on the Creative Studies Project, **Toward Supersanity, Channeled Freedom** (Out-of-print), authored in 1973 by my colleague Ruth B. Noller and me. It also draws from papers I have presented at national and international research conferences, as well as from a number of articles I wrote with various psychologists during these years of scientific evaluations of programs and methods for nurturing creative talent.

The article contains five sections: (a) a brief overview of the international research on deliberate cultivation of creative abilities; (b) a concise review of the early creativity research at State University at Buffalo; (c) a brief summary of the findings of the Creative Studies Project which comprehensively evaluated a four-semester sequence of developmental courses at the college level; (d) a detailed "case study" of the Project, its research methods, results and implications; (e) further research questions suggested by the Project.

4. Parnes, S. J. "CPSI: The General System." *Journal Of Creative Behavior,* 1977, 11 (1).

This article provides a theoretical, general-systems basis for the creative problem-solving processes of the present book. The *Journal Of Creative Behavior* is a quarterly designed for the serious general reader in the field. It provides a continuous flow of pertinent information, research, developments, applications, literature, etc. It is published by The Creative Education Foundation, Inc.

Index